Dragon's Blood

Henry Milner Rideout

Alpha Editions

This edition published in 2021

ISBN : 9789355342829

Design and Setting By
Alpha Editions
www.alphaedis.com
Email - info@alphaedis.com

Contents

CHAPTER I   - 1 -

A LADY AND A GRIFFIN   - 1 -

CHAPTER II   - 10 -

THE PIED PIPER   - 10 -

CHAPTER III   - 19 -

UNDER FIRE   - 19 -

CHAPTER IV   - 28 -

THE SWORD-PEN   - 28 -

CHAPTER V   - 35 -

IN TOWN   - 35 -

CHAPTER VI   - 43 -

THE PAGODA   - 43 -

CHAPTER VII   - 51 -

IPHIGENIA   - 51 -

CHAPTER VIII   - 59 -

THE HOT NIGHT   - 59 -

CHAPTER IX   - 67 -

PASSAGE AT ARMS   - 67 -

CHAPTER X   - 77 -

THREE PORTALS   - 77 -

CHAPTER XI   - 84 -

WHITE LOTUS   - 84 -

CHAPTER XII   - 93 -

THE WAR BOARD   - 93 -

CHAPTER XIII   - 102 -

THE SPARE MAN   - 102 -

CHAPTER XIV   - 110 -

OFF DUTY   - 110 -

CHAPTER XV   - 118 -

KAU FAI   - 118 -

CHAPTER XVI   - 126 -

THE GUNWALE   - 126 -

CHAPTER XVII   - 134 -

LAMP OF HEAVEN   - 134 -

CHAPTER XVIII   - 141 -

SIEGE   - 141 -

CHAPTER XIX   - 150 -

BROTHER MOLES   - 150 -

CHAPTER XX   - 158 -

THE HAKKA BOAT   - 158 -

CHAPTER XXI   - 166 -

THE DRAGON'S SHADOW   - 166 -

CHAPTER I

A LADY AND A GRIFFIN

It was "about first-drink time," as the captain of the Tsuen-Chau, bound for Shanghai and Japan ports, observed to his friend Cesare Domenico, a good British subject born at Malta. They sat on the coolest corner in Port Said, their table commanding both the cross-way of Chareh Sultan el Osman, and the short, glaring vista of desert dust and starved young acacias which led to the black hulks of shipping in the Canal. From the Bar la Poste came orchestral strains--"Ai nostri monti"--performed by a piano indoors and two violins on the pavement. The sounds contended with a thin, scattered strumming of cafe mandolins, the tinkle of glasses, the steady click of dominoes and backgammon; then were drowned in the harsh chatter of Arab coolies who, all grimed as black as Nubians, and shouldering spear-headed shovels, tramped inland, their long tunics stiff with coal-dust, like a band of chain-mailed Crusaders lately caught in a hurricane of powdered charcoal. Athwart them, Parisian gowns floated past on stout Italian forms; hulking third-class Australians, in shirtsleeves, slouched along toward their mail-boat, hugging whiskey bottles, baskets of oranges, baskets of dates; British soldiers, khaki-clad for India, raced galloping donkeys through the crowded and dusty street. It was mail-day, and gayety flowed among the tables, under the thin acacias, on a high tide of Amer Picon.

Through the inky files of the coaling-coolies burst an alien and bewildered figure. He passed unnoticed, except by the filthy little Arab bootblacks who swarmed about him, trotting, capering, yelping cheerfully: "Mista Ferguson!--polish, finish!--can-can--see nice Frencha girl--Mista McKenzie, Scotcha fella from Dublin--smotta picture--polish, finish!"--undertoned by a squabbling chorus. But presently, studying his face, they cried in a loud voice, "Nix! Alles!" and left him, as one not desiring polish.

"German, that chap," drawled the captain of the Tsuen-

Chau, lazily, noticing the uncertain military walk of the young man's clumsy legs, his uncouth clothes, his pale visage winged by blushing ears of coral pink.

"The Eitel's in, then," replied Cesare. And they let the young Teuton vanish in the vision of mixed lives.

Down the lane of music and chatter and drink he passed slowly, like a man just wakened,--assailed by Oriental noise and smells, jostled by the races of all latitudes and longitudes, surrounded and solitary, unheeded and self-conscious. With a villager's awkwardness among crowds, he made his way to a German shipping-office.

"Dispatches for Rudolph Hackh?" he inquired, twisting up his blond moustache, and trying to look insolent and peremptory, like an employer of men.

"There are none, sir," answered an amiable clerk, not at all impressed.

Abashed once more in the polyglot street, still daunted by his first plunge into the foreign and the strange, he retraced his path, threading shyly toward the Quai François Joseph. He slipped through the barrier gate, signaled clumsily to a boatman, crawled under the drunken little awning of the dinghy, and steered a landsman's course along the shining Canal toward the black wall of a German mail-boat. Cramping the Arab's oar along the iron side, he bumped the landing-stage. Safe on deck, he became in a moment stiff and haughty, greeting a fellow passenger here and there with a half-military salute. All afternoon he sat or walked alone, unapproachable, eyeing with a fierce and gloomy stare the squalid front of wooden houses on the African side, the gray desert glare of Asia, the pale blue ribbon of the great Canal stretching southward into the unknown.

He composed melancholy German verses in a note-book. He recalled famous exiles--Camoens, Napoleon, Byron--and essayed to copy something of all three in his attitude. He cherished the thought that he, clerk at twenty-one, was now agent at twenty-two, and traveling toward a house with servants, off there beyond the turn of the Canal, beyond the curve of the globe. But for all this, Rudolph Hackh felt young, homesick, timid of the future, and already oppressed with the distance, the age, the manifold, placid mystery of

China.

Toward that mystery, meanwhile, the ship began to creep.
Behind her, houses, multi-colored funnels, scrubby trees,
slowly swung to blot out the glowing Mediterranean and the
western hemisphere. Gray desert banks closed in upon her
strictly, slid gently astern, drawing with them to the
vanishing-point the bright lane of traversed water. She
gained the Bitter Lakes; and the red conical buoys, like
beads a-stringing, slipped on and added to the two
converging dotted lines.

"Good-by to the West!" thought Rudolph. As he mourned
sentimentally at this lengthening tally of their departure, and
tried to quote appropriate farewells, he was deeply touched
and pleased by the sadness of his emotions. "Now what
does Byron say?"

The sombre glow of romantic sentiment faded, however,
with the sunset. That evening, as the ship glided from ruby
coal to ruby coal of the gares, following at a steady six knots
the theatric glare of her search-light along arsenically green
cardboard banks, Rudolph paced the deck in a mood much
simpler and more honest. In vain he tried the half-baked
philosophy of youth. It gave no comfort; and watching the
clear desert stars of two mysterious continents, he fell prey
to the unbounded and unintelligible complexity of man's
world. His own career seemed no more dubious than trivial.

Succeeding days only strengthened this mood. The Red Sea
passed in a dream of homesickness, intolerable heat, of a
pale blue surface stretched before aching eyes, and paler
strips of pink and gray coast, faint and distant. Like dreams,
too, passed Aden and Colombo; and then, suddenly, he
woke to the most acute interest.

He had ignored his mess-mates at their second-class table;
but when the new passengers from Colombo came to
dinner, he heard behind him the swish of stiff skirts, felt
some one brush his shoulder, and saw, sliding into the next
revolving chair, the vision of a lady in white.

"*Mahlzeit*" she murmured dutifully. But the voice was not
German. Rudolph heard her subside with little flouncings,
and felt his ears grow warm and red. Delighted,
embarrassed, he at last took sufficient courage to steal side-

glances.

The first showed her to be young, fair-haired, and smartly attired in the plainest and coolest of white; the second, not so young, but very charming, with a demure downcast look, and a deft control of her spoon that, to Rudolph's eyes, was splendidly fastidious; at the third, he was shocked to encounter the last flitting light of a counter-glance, from large, dark-blue eyes, not devoid of amusement.

"She laughs at me!" fumed the young man, inwardly. He was angry, conscious of those unlucky wing-and-wing ears, vexed at his own boldness. "I have been offensive. She laughs at me." He generalized from long inexperience of a subject to which he had given acutely interested thought: "They always do."

Anger did not prevent him, however, from noting that his neighbor traveled alone, that she must be an Englishwoman, and yet that she diffused, somehow, an aura of the Far East and of romance. He shot many a look toward her deck-chair that evening, and when she had gone below, strategically bought a cigar, sat down in the chair to light it, and by a carefully shielded match contrived to read the tag that fluttered on the arm: "B. Forrester, Hongkong."

Afterward he remembered that by early daylight he might have read it for nothing; and so, for economic penance, smoked to the bitter end, finding the cigar disagreeable but manly. At all events, homesickness had vanished in a curious impatience for the morrow. Miss Forrester: he would sit beside Miss Forrester at table. If only they both were traveling first-class!--then she might be a great lady. To be enamored of a countess, now--A cigar, after all, was the proper companion of bold thoughts.

At breakfast, recalling her amusement, he remained silent and wooden. At tiffin his heart leaped.

"You speak English, I'm sure, don't you?" Miss Forrester was saying, in a pleasant, rather drawling voice. Her eyes were quite serious now, and indeed friendly. Confusion seized him.

"I have less English to amuse myself with the ladies," he answered wildly. Next moment, however, he regained that painful mastery of the tongue which had won his promotion as agent, and stammered: "Pardon. I would mean, I speak so badly as not to entertain her."

"Indeed, you speak very nicely," she rejoined, with such a smile as no woman had ever troubled to bestow on him. "That will be so pleasant, for my German is shocking."

Dazed by the compliment, by her manner of taking for granted that future conversation which had seemed too good to come true, but above all by her arch, provoking smile, Rudolph sat with his head in a whirl, feeling that the wide eyes of all the second-cabiners were penetrating the tumultuous secret of his breast. Again his English deserted, and left him stammering. But Miss Forrester chatted steadily, appeared to understand murmurs which he himself found obscure, and so restored his confidence that before tiffin was over he talked no less gayly, his honest face alight and glowing. She taught him the names of the strange fruits before them; but though listening and questioning eagerly, he could not afterward have told loquat from pumelo, or custard-apple from papaya.

Nor could this young man, of methodical habits, ever have told how long their voyage lasted. It passed, unreal and timeless, in a glorious mist, a delighted fever: the background a blur of glossy white bulkheads and iron rails, awnings that fluttered in the warm, languorous winds, an infinite tropic ocean poignantly blue; the foreground, Miss Forrester. Her white figure, trim and dashing; her round blue eyes, filled with coy wonder, the arch innocence of a spoiled child; her pale, smooth cheeks, rather plump, but coming oddly and enticingly to a point at the mouth and tilted chin; her lips, somewhat too full, too red, but quick and whimsical: he saw these all, and these only, in a bright focus, listening meanwhile to a voice by turns languid and lively, with now and then a curious liquid softness, perhaps insincere, yet dangerously pleasant. Questioning, hinting, she played at motherly age and wisdom. As for him, he never before knew how well he could talk, or how engrossing his sober life, both in his native village on the Baltic and afterward in Bremen, could prove to either himself or a stranger.

Yet he was not such a fool, he reflected, as to tell

everything. So far from trading confidences, she had told him only that she was bound straight on to Hongkong; that curiosity alone had led her to travel second-class, "for the delightful change, you know, from all such formality"; and that she was "really more French than English." Her reticence had the charm of an incognito; and taking this leaf from her book, he gave himself out as a large, vaguely important person journeying on a large, vague errand.

"But you are a griffin?" she had said, as they sat together at tea.

"Pardon?" he ventured, wary and alarmed, wondering whether he could claim this unknown term as in character with his part.

"I mean," Miss Forrester explained, smiling, "it is your first visit to the Far East?"

"Oh, yes," he replied eagerly, blushing. He would have given worlds to say, "No."

"Griffins are such nice little monsters," she purred. "I like them."

Sometimes at night, waked by the snores of a fat Prussian in the upper berth, he lay staring into the dark, while the ship throbbed in unison with his excited thoughts. He was amazed at his happy recklessness. He would never see her again; he was hurrying toward lonely and uncertain shores; yet this brief voyage outvalued the rest of his life.

In time, they had left Penang,--another unheeded background for her arch, innocent, appealing face,--and forged down the Strait of Malacca in a flood of nebulous moonlight. It was the last night out from Singapore. That veiled brightness, as they leaned on the rail, showed her brown hair fluttering dimly, her face pale, half real, half magical, her eyes dark and undefined pools of mystery. It was late; they had been silent for a long time; and Rudolph felt that something beyond the territory of words remained to be said, and that the one brilliant epoch of his life now drew madly to a close.

"What do you think of it all?" the woman asked suddenly, gravely, as though they had been isolated together in the deep spaces of the same thought.

"I do not yet--Of what?" rejoined Rudolph, at a loss.

"Of all this." She waved an eloquent little gesture toward the azure-lighted gulf.

"Oh," he said. "Of the world?"

"Yes," she answered slowly. "The world. Life." Her tone, subdued and musical, conveyed in the mere words their full enigma and full meaning. "All this that we see."

"Who can tell?" He took her seriously, and ransacked all his store of second-hand philosophy for a worthy answer,--a musty store, dead and pedantic, after the thrilling spirit of her words. "Why, I think--it is--is it not all now the sense-manifest substance of our duty? Pardon. I am obscure. '*Das versinnlichte Material unserer Pflicht*' No?"

Her clear laughter startled him.

"Oh, how moral!" she cried. "What a highly moral little griffin!"

She laughed again (but this time it was like the splash of water in a deep well), and turned toward him that curiously tilted point of chin and mouth, her eyes shadowy and mocking. She looked young again,--the spirit of youth, of knowledge, of wonderful brightness and unbelief.

"Must we take it so very, very hard?" she coaxed. "Isn't it just a place to be happy in?"

As through a tumult he heard, and recognized the wisdom of the ages.

"Because," she added, "it lasts such a little while--"

On the rail their hands suddenly touched. He was aware of nothing but the nearness and pallor of her face, the darkness of her eyes shining up at him. All his life seemed to have rushed concentrating into that one instant of extreme trouble, happiness, trembling fascination.

Footsteps sounded on the deck behind them; an unwelcome voice called jocosely:--

"Good efening!" The ship's doctor advanced with a roguish, paternal air. "You see at the phosphor, not?"

Even as she whipped about toward the light, Rudolph had seen, with a touch of wonder, how her face changed from a bitter frown to the most friendly smile. The frown returned, became almost savage, when the fat physician continued:--

"To see the phosphor is too much moon, Mrs. Forrester?"

Had the steamer crashed upon a reef, he would hardly have noticed such a minor shipwreck. Mrs. Forrester? why, then-- When the doctor, after ponderous pleasantries, had waddled away aft, Rudolph turned upon her a face of tragedy.

"Was that true?" he demanded grimly.

"Was what true?" she asked, with baby eyes of wonder, which no longer deceived, but angered.

"What the doctor said." Rudolph's voice trembled. "The tittle--the title he gave you."

"Why, of course," she laughed.

"And you did not tell me!" he began, with scorn.

"Don't be foolish," she cut in. From beneath her skirt the toe of a small white shoe tapped the deck angrily. Of a sudden she laughed, and raised a tantalizing face, merry, candid, and inscrutable. "Why, you never asked me, and-- and of course I thought you were saying it all along. You have such a dear, funny way of pronouncing, you know."

He hesitated, almost believing; then, with a desperate gesture, wheeled and marched resolutely aft. That night it was no Prussian snores which kept him awake and wretched. "Everything is finished," he thought abysmally. He lay overthrown, aching, crushed, as though pinned under the fallen walls of his youth.

At breakfast-time, the ship lay still beside a quay where mad crowds of brown and yellow men, scarfed, swathed, and turbaned in riotous colors, worked quarreling with harsh cries, in unspeakable interweaving uproar. The air, hot and steamy, smelled of strange earth. As Rudolph followed a Malay porter toward the gang-plank, he was painfully aware that Mrs. Forrester had turned from the rail and stood waiting in his path.

"Without saying good-by?" she reproached him. The injured

wonder in her eyes he thought a little overdone.

"Good-by." He could not halt, but, raising his cap stiffly, managed to add, "A pleasant voyage," and passed on, feeling as though she had murdered something.

He found himself jogging in a rickshaw, while equatorial rain beat like down-pouring bullets on the tarpaulin hood, and sluiced the Chinaman's oily yellow back. Over the heavy-muscled shoulders he caught glimpses of sullen green foliage, ponderous and drooping; of half-naked barbarians that squatted in the shallow caverns of shops; innumerable faces, black, yellow, white, and brown, whirling past, beneath other tarpaulin hoods, or at carriage windows, or shielded by enormous dripping wicker hats, or bared to the pelting rain. Curious odors greeted him, as of sour vegetables and of unknown rank substances burning. He stared like a visionary at the streaming multitude of alien shapes.

The coolie swerved, stopped, tilted his shafts to the ground. Rudolph entered a sombre, mouldy office, where the darkness rang with tiny silver bells. Pig-tailed men in skull-caps, their faces calm as polished ivory, were counting dollars endlessly over flying finger-tips. One of these men paused long enough to give him a sealed dispatch,--the message to which the ocean-bed, the Midgard ooze, had thrilled beneath his tardy keel.

"Zimmerman recalled," the interpretation ran; "take his station; proceed at once."

He knew the port only as forlorn and insignificant. It did not matter. One consolation remained: he would never see her again.

CHAPTER II

THE PIED PIPER

A gray smudge trailing northward showed where the Fa-Hien--Scottish Oriental, sixteen hundred tons--was disappearing from the pale expanse of ocean. The sampan drifted landward imperceptibly, seeming, with nut-brown sail unstirred, to remain where the impatient steamer had met it, dropped a solitary passenger overside, and cast him loose upon the breadth of the antipodes. Rare and far, the sails of junks patched the horizon with umber polygons. Rudolph, sitting among his boxes in the sampan, viewed by turns this desolate void astern and the more desolate sweep of coast ahead. His matting sail divided the shining bronze outpour of an invisible river, divided a low brown shore beyond, and above these, the strips of some higher desert country that shone like snowdrifts, or like sifted ashes from which the hills rose black and charred. Their savage, winter-blasted look, in the clear light of an almost vernal morning, made the land seem fabulous. Yet here in reality, thought Rudolph, as he floated toward that hoary kingdom,--here at last, facing a lonely sea, reared the lifeless, inhospitable shore, the sullen margin of China.

The slow creaking of the spliced oar, swung in its lashing by a half-naked yellow man, his incomprehensible chatter with some fellow boatman hidden in the bows, were sounds lost in a drowsy silence, rhythms lost in a wide inertia. Time itself seemed stationary. Rudolph nodded, slept, and waking, found the afternoon sped, the hills gone, and his clumsy, time-worn craft stealing close under a muddy bank topped with brown weeds and grass. They had left behind the silted roadstead, and now, gliding on a gentle flood, entered the river-mouth. Here and there, against the saffron tide, or under banks quaggy as melting chocolate, stooped a naked fisherman, who--swarthy as his background but for a loin-band of yellow flesh--shone wet and glistening while he stirred a dip-net through the liquid mud. Faint in the distance harsh cries sounded now and then, and the soft popping of small-arms,--tiny revolts in the reign of a stillness aged and formidable. Crumbling walls and squat ruins, black and green-patched with mould--old towers of defense against pirates--guarded from either bank the turns of the river. In one reach, a "war-junk," her sails furled, lay at anchor, the red and white eyes staring fish-like from her black prow: a silly monster, the painted tompions of her wooden cannon aiming drunkenly askew, her crew's wash fluttering peacefully in a line of blue dungaree.

Beyond the next turn, a fowling-piece cracked sharply, close at hand; something splashed, and the ruffled body of a snipe bobbed in the bronze flood alongside.

"Hang it!" complained a voice, loudly. "The beggar was too--Hallo! Oh, I say, Gilly! Gilly, ahoy! Pick us up, there 's a good chap! The bird first, will you, and then me."

A tall young man in brown holland and a battered *terai* stood above on the grassy brink.

"Oh, beg pardon," he continued. "Took you for old Gilly, you know." He snapped the empty shells from his gun, and blew into the breech, before adding, "Would *you* mind, then? That is, if you're bound up for Stink-Chau. It's a beastly long tramp, and I've been shooting all afternoon."

Followed by three coolies who popped out of the grass with game-bags, the young stranger descended, hopped nimbly from tussock to gunwale, and perched there to wash his boots in the river.

"Might have known you weren't old Gilly," he said over his shoulder. "Wutzler said the Fa-Hien lay off signaling for sampan before breakfast. Going to stay long?"

"I am agent," answered Rudolph, with a touch of pride, "for Fliegelman and Sons."

"Oh?" drawled the hunter, lazily. He swung his legs inboard, faced about, and studied Rudolph with embarrassing frankness. He was a long-limbed young Englishman, whose cynical gray eyes, and thin face tinged rather sallow and Oriental, bespoke a reckless good humor. "Life sentence, eh? Then your name's--what is it again?--Hackh, isn't it? Heywood's mine. So you take Zimmerman's place. He's off already, and good riddance. He *was* a bounder!--Charming spot you've come to! I daresay if your Fliegelmans opened a hong in hell, you might possibly get a worse station."

Without change of manner, he uttered a few gabbling, barbaric words. A coolie knelt, and with a rag began to clean the boots, which, from the expression of young Mr. Heywood's face, were more interesting than the arrival of a new manager from Germany.

"It will be dark before we're in," he said. "My place for the night, of course, and let your predecessor's leavings stand over till daylight. After dinner we'll go to the club. Dinner! Chicken and rice, chicken and rice! Better like it, though, for you'll eat nothing else, term of your life."

"You are very kind," began Rudolph; but this bewildering off-hand youngster cut him short, with a laugh:--

"No fear, you'll pay me! Your firm supplies unlimited liquor. Much good that ever did us, with old Zimmerman."

The sampan now slipped rapidly on the full flood, up a narrow channel that the setting of the sun had turned, as at a blow, from copper to indigo. The shores passed, more and more obscure against a fading light. A star or two already shone faint in the lower spaces. A second war-junk loomed above them, with a ruddy fire in the stern lighting a glimpse of squat forms and yellow goblin faces.

"It is very curious," said Rudolph, trying polite conversation, "how they paint so the eyes on their jonks."

"No eyes, no can see; no can see, no can walkee," chanted Heywood in careless formula. "I say," he complained suddenly, "you're not going to 'study the people,' and all that rot? We're already fed up with missionaries. Their cant, I mean; no allusion to cannibalism."

He lighted a cigarette. After the blinding flare of the match, night seemed to have fallen instantaneously. As their boat crept on to the slow creaking sweep, both maintained silence, Rudolph rebuked and lonely, Heywood supine beneath a comfortable winking spark.

"What I mean is," drawled the hunter, "we need all the good fellows we can get. Bring any new songs out? Oh, I forgot, you're a German, too.--A sweet little colony! Gilly's the only gentleman in the whole half-dozen of us, and Heaven knows he's not up to much.--Ah, we're in. On our right, fellow sufferers, we see the blooming Village of Stinks."

He had risen in the gloom. Beyond his shadow a few feeble lights burned low and scattered along the bank. Strange cries arose, the bumping of sampans, the mournful caterwauling of a stringed instrument.

"The native town's a bit above," he continued. "We herd together here on the edge. No concession, no bund, nothing."

Their sampan grounded softly in malodorous ooze. Each mounting the bare shoulders of a coolie, the two Europeans rode precariously to shore.

"My boys will fetch your boxes," called Heywood. "Come on."

The path, sometimes marshy, sometimes hard-packed clay or stone flags deeply littered, led them a winding course in the night. Now and then shapes met them and pattered past in single file, furtive and sinister. At last, where a wall loomed white, Heywood stopped, and, kicking at a wooden gate, gave a sing-song cry. With rattling weights, the door swung open, and closed behind them heavily. A kind of empty garden, a bare little inclosure, shone dimly in the light that streamed from a low, thick-set veranda at the farther end. Dogs flew at them, barking outrageously.

"Down, Chang! Down, Chutney!" cried their master. "Be quiet, Flounce, you fool!"

On the stone floor of the house, they leaped upon him, two red chows and a fox-terrier bitch, knocking each other over in their joy.

"Olo she-dog he catchee plenty lats," piped a little Chinaman, who shuffled out from a side-room where lamplight showed an office desk. "Too-day catchee. Plenty lats. No can."

"My compradore, Ah Pat," said Heywood to Rudolph. "Ah Pat, my friend he b'long number one Flickleman, boss man."

The withered little creature bobbed in his blue robe,

grinning at the introduction.

"You welly high-tone man," he murmured amiably.
"Catchee goo' plice."

"All the same, I don't half like it," was Heywood's comment
later. He had led his guest upstairs into a bare white-washed
room, furnished in wicker. Open windows admitted the
damp sea breeze and a smell, like foul gun-barrels, from the
river marshes. "Where should all the rats be coming from?"
He frowned, meditating on what Rudolph thought a trifle.
Above the sallow brown face, his chestnut hair shone oddly,
close-cropped and vigorous. "Maskee, can't be helped.--O
Boy, one sherry-bitters, one bamboo!"

"To our better acquaintance," said Rudolph, as they raised
their glasses.

"What? Oh, yes, thanks," the other laughed. "Any one
would know you for a griffin here, Mr. Hackh. You've not
forgotten your manners yet."

When they had sat down to dinner in another white-washed
room, and had undertaken the promised rice and chicken,
he laughed again, somewhat bitterly.

"Better acquaintance--no fear! You'll be so well acquainted
with us all that you'll wish you never clapped eyes on us."
He drained his whiskey and soda, signaled for more, and
added: "Were you ever cooped up, yachting, with a chap you
detested? That's the feeling you come to have.--Here, stand
by. You're drinking nothing."

Rudolph protested. Politeness had so far conquered habit,
that he felt uncommonly flushed, genial, and giddy.

"That," urged Heywood, tapping the bottle, "that's our only
amusement. You'll see. One good thing we can get is the
liquor. 'Nisi damnose bibimus,'--forget how it runs:" Drink
hearty, or you'll die without getting your revenge,'"

"You are then a university's-man?" cried Rudolph, with
enthusiasm.

The other nodded gloomily. On the instant his face had
fallen as impassive as that of the Chinese boy who stood
behind his chair, straight, rigid, like a waxen image of
Gravity in a blue gown.--"Yes, of sorts. Young fool. Scrapes.

Debt. Out to Orient. Same old story. More debt. Trust the firm to encourage that! Debt and debt and debt. Tied up safe. Transfer. Finish! Never go Home."--He rose with a laugh and an impatient gesture.--"Come on. Might as well take in the club as to sit here talking rot."

Outside the gate of the compound, coolies crouching round a lantern sprang upright and whipped a pair of sedan-chairs into position. Heywood, his feet elevated comfortably over the poles, swung in the lead; Rudolph followed, bobbing in the springy rhythm of the long bamboos. The lanterns danced before them down an open road, past a few blank walls and dark buildings, and soon halted before a whitened front, where light gleamed from the upper story.

"Mind the stairs," called Heywood. "Narrow and beastly dark."

As they stumbled up the steep flight, Rudolph heard the click of billiard balls. A pair of hanging lamps lighted the room into which he rose,--a low, gloomy loft, devoid of comfort. At the nearer table, a weazened little man bent eagerly over a pictorial paper; at the farther, chalking their cues, stood two players, one a sturdy Englishman with a gray moustache, the other a lithe, graceful person, whose blue coat, smart as an officer's, and swarthy but handsome face made him at a glance the most striking figure in the room. A little Chinese imp in white, who acted as marker, turned on the new-comers a face of preternatural cunning.

"Mr. Wutzler," said Heywood. The weazened reader rose in a nervous flutter, underwent his introduction to Rudolph with as much bashful agony as a school-girl, mumbled a few words in German, and instantly took refuge in his tattered *Graphic*. The players, however, advanced in a more friendly fashion. The Englishman, whose name Rudolph did not catch, shook his hand heartily.

"Mr. Hackh is a welcome addition." He spoke with deliberate courtesy. Something in his voice, the tired look in his frank blue eyes and serious face, at once engaged respect. "For our sakes," he continued, "we're glad to see you here. I am sure Doctor Chantel will agree with me."

"Ah, indeed," said the man in military blue, with a courtier's bow. Both air and accent were French. "Most welcome."

"Let's all have a drink," cried Heywood. Despite his many glasses at dinner, he spoke with the alacrity of a new idea. "O Boy, whiskey *Ho-lan suey, fai di*!"

Away bounded the boy marker like a tennis-ball.

"Hello, Wutzler's off already!"--The little old reader had quietly disappeared, leaving them a vacant table.--"Isn't he weird?" laughed Heywood, as they sat down. "Comes and goes like a ghost."

"It is his Chinese wife," declared Chantel, preening his moustache. "He is always ashame to meet the new persons."

"Poor old chap," said Heywood. "I know--feels himself an outcast and all that. Humph! With us! Quite unnecessary."-- The Chinese page, quick, solemn, and noiseless, glided round the table with his tray.--"Ah, you young devil! You're another weird one, you atom. See those bead eyes watching us, eh? A Gilpin Homer, you are, and some fine day we'll see you go off in a flash of fire. If you don't poison us all first.--Well, here's fortune!"

"Your health, Mr. Hackh," amended the other Englishman.

As they set down their glasses, a strange cry sounded from below,--a stifled call, inarticulate, but in such a key of distress that all four faced about, and listened intently.

"Kom down," called a hesitating voice, "kom down and look-see."

They sprang to the stairs, and clattered downward. Dim radiance flooded the landing, from the street door. Outside, a smoky lantern on the ground revealed the lower levels.

In the wide sector of light stood Wutzler, shrinking and apologetic, like a man caught in a fault, his wrinkled face eloquent of fear, his gesture eloquent of excuse. Round him, as round a conjurer, scores of little shadowy things moved in a huddling dance, fitfully hopping like sparrows over spilt grain. Where the light fell brightest these became plainer, their eyes shone in jeweled points of color.

"By Jove, Gilly, they are rats!" said Heywood, in a voice curiously forced and matter-of-fact. "Flounce killed several this afternoon, so my--"

No one heeded him; all stared. The rats, like beings of incantation, stole about with an absence of fear, a disregard of man's presence, that was odious and alarming.

"Earthquake?" The elder Englishman spoke as though afraid of disturbing some one.

The French doctor shook his head.

"No," he answered in the same tone. "Look."

The rats, in all their weaving confusion, displayed one common impulse. They sprang upward continually, with short, agonized leaps, like drowning creatures struggling to keep afloat above some invisible flood. The action, repeated multitudinously into the obscure background, exaggerated in the foreground by magnified shadows tossing and falling on the white walls, suggested the influence of some evil stratum, some vapor subtle and diabolic, crawling poisonously along the ground.

Heywood stamped angrily, without effect. Wutzler stood abject, a magician impotent against his swarm of familiars. Gradually the rats, silent and leaping, passed away into the darkness, as though they heard the summons of a Pied Piper.

"It doesn't attack Europeans." Heywood still used that curious inflection.

"Then my brother Julien is still alive," retorted Doctor Chantel, bitterly.

"What do you think, Gilly?" persisted Heywood.

His compatriot nodded in a meaningless way.

"The doctor's right, of course," he answered. "I wish my wife weren't coming back."

"Dey are a remember," ventured Wutzler, timidly. "A warnung."

The others, as though it had been a point of custom, ignored him. All stared down, musing, at the vacant stones.

"Then the concert's off to-morrow night," mocked Heywood, with an unpleasant laugh.

"On the contrary." Gilly caught him up, prompt and decided. "We shall need all possible amusements; also to meet and plan our campaign. Meantime,--what do you say, Doctor?--chloride of lime in pots?"

"That, evidently," smiled the handsome man. "Yes, and charcoal burnt in braziers, perhaps, as Père Fenouil advises. Fumigate."--Satirical and debonair, he shrugged his shoulders.--"What use, among these thousands of yellow pigs?"

"I wish she weren't coming," repeated Gilly.

Rudolph, left outside this conference, could bear the uncertainty no longer.

"I am a new arrival," he confided to his young host. "I do not understand. What is it?"

"The plague, old chap," replied Heywood, curtly. "These playful little animals get first notice. You're not the only arrival to-night."

CHAPTER III

UNDER FIRE

The desert was sometimes Gobi, sometimes Sahara, but always an infinite stretch of sand that floated up and up in a stifling layer, like the tide. Rudolph, desperately choked, continued leaping upward against an insufferable power of gravity, or straining to run against the force of paralysis. The desert rang with phantom voices,--Chinese voices that mocked him, chanting of pestilence, intoning abhorrently in French.

He woke to find a knot of bed-clothes smothering him. To his first unspeakable relief succeeded the astonishment of hearing the voices continue in shrill chorus, the tones Chinese, the words, in louder fragments, unmistakably French. They sounded close at hand, discordant matins sung by a mob of angry children. Once or twice a weary, fretful voice scolded feebly: "Un-peu-de-s'lence! Un-peu-de-s'lence!" Rudolph rose to peep through the heavy jalousies, but saw nothing more than sullen daylight, a flood of vertical rain, and thin rivulets coursing down a tiled roof below. The morning was dismally cold.

"Jolivet's kids wake you?" Heywood, in a blue kimono, nodded from the doorway. "Public nuisance, that school. Quite needless, too. Some bally French theory, you know, sphere of influence, and that rot. Game played out up here, long ago, but they keep hanging on.--Bath's ready, when you like." He broke out laughing. "Did you climb into the water-jar, yesterday, before dinner? Boy reports it upset. You'll find the dipper more handy.--How did you ever manage? One leg at a time?"

Echoes of glee followed his disappearance. Rudolph, blushing, prepared to descend into the gloomy vault of ablution. Charcoal fumes, however, and the glow of a brazier on the dark floor below, not only revived all his old terror, but at the stair-head halted him with a new.

"Is the water safe?" he called.

Heywood answered impatiently from his bedroom.

"Nothing safe in this world, Mr. Hackh. User's risk." An inaudible mutter ended with, "Keep clean, anyway."

At breakfast, though the acrid smoke was an enveloping reminder, he made the only reference to their situation.

"Rain at last: too late, though, to flush out the gutters. We needed it a month ago.--I say, Hackh, if you don't mind, you might as well cheer up. From now on, it's pure heads and tails. We're all under fire together." Glancing out of window at the murky sky, he added thoughtfully, "One excellent side to living without hope, maskee fashion: one isn't specially afraid. I'll take you to your office, and you can make a start. Nothing else to do, is there?"

Dripping bearers and shrouded chairs received them on the lower floor, carried them out into a chill rain that drummed overhead and splashed along the compound path in silver points. The sunken flags in the road formed a narrow aqueduct that wavered down a lane of mire. A few grotesque wretches, thatched about with bamboo matting, like bottles, or like rosebushes in winter, trotted past shouldering twin baskets. The smell of joss-sticks, fish, and sour betel, the subtle sweetness of opium, grew constantly stronger, blended with exhalations of ancient refuse, and (as the chairs jogged past the club, past filthy groups huddling about the well in a marketplace, and onward into the black yawn of the city gate) assailed the throat like a bad and lasting taste. Now, in the dusky street, pent narrowly by wet stone walls, night seemed to fall, while fresh waves of pungent odor overwhelmed and steeped the senses. Rudolph's chair jostled through hundreds and hundreds of Chinese, all alike in the darkness, who shuffled along before with switching queues, or flattened against the wall to stare, almost nose to nose, at the passing foreigner. With chairpoles backing into one shop or running ahead into another, with raucous cries from the coolies, he swung round countless corners, bewildered in a dark, leprous, nightmare bazaar. Overhead, a slit of cloudy sky showed rarely; for the most part, he swayed along indoors, beneath a dingy lattice roof. All points of the compass vanished; all streets remained alike,--the same endless vista of mystic characters, red, black, and gold, on narrow suspended tablets, under which flowed the same current of pig-tailed men in blue and dirty white. From every shop, the same yellow faces stared at him, the same elfin children caught his eye for a half-second to grin or grimace, the same shaven foreheads bent over microscopical tasks in the dark. At first, Rudolph thought the city loud and brawling; but resolving this impression to the hideous shouts of his coolies parting the crowd, he detected, below or through their noise, from all the long cross-corridors a wide and appalling silence. Gradually, too, small sounds relieved this: the hammering of brass-work, the steady rattle of a loom, or the sing-song call and mellow bell of some burdened hawker, bumping past, his swinging baskets filled with a pennyworth of trifles. But still the silence daunted Rudolph in this astounding vision, this masque of unreal life, of lost daylight, of annihilated direction, of placid turmoil and multifarious identity, made credible only by the permanence of nauseous smells.

Somewhere in the dark maze, the chairs halted, under a portal black and heavy as a Gate of Dreams. And as by the anachronism of dreams there hung, among its tortuous symbols, the small, familiar placard--"Fliegelman and Sons, Office." Heywood led the way, past two ducking Chinese clerks, into a sombre room, stone-floored, furnished stiffly with a row of carved chairs against the wall, lighted coldly by roof-windows of placuna, and a lamp smoking before some commercial god in his ebony and tinsel shrine.

"There," he said, bringing Rudolph to an inner chamber, or dark little pent-house, where another draughty lamp flickered on a European desk. "Here's your cell. I'm off--call for you later. Good luck!"--Wheeling in the doorway, he tossed a book, negligently.--"Caught! You may as well start in, eh?--'Cantonese Made Worse,'"

To his departing steps Rudolph listened as a prisoner, condemned, might listen to the last of all earthly visitors. Peering through a kind of butler's window, he saw beyond the shrine his two pallid subordinates, like mystic automatons, nodding and smoking by the doorway. Beyond them, across a darker square like a cavern-mouth, flitted the living phantoms of the street. It seemed a fit setting for his fears. "I am lost," he thought; lost among goblins, marooned in the age of barbarism, shut in a labyrinth with a

Black Death at once actual and mediaeval: he dared not think of Home, but flung his arms on the littered desk, and buried his face.

On the tin pent-roof, the rain trampled inexorably.

At last, mustering a shaky resolution, he set to work ransacking the tumbled papers. Happily, Zimmerman had left all in confusion. The very hopelessness of his accounts proved a relief. Working at high tension, Rudolph wrestled through disorder, mistakes, falsification; and little by little, as the sorted piles grew and his pen traveled faster, the old absorbing love of method and dispatch--the stay, the cordial flagon of troubled man--gave him strength to forget.

At times, felt shoes scuffed the stone floor without, and high, scolding voices rose, exchanging unfathomable courtesy with his clerks. One after another, strange figures, plump and portly in their colored robes, crossed his threshold, nodding their buttoned caps, clasping their hands hidden in voluminous sleeves.

"My 'long speakee my goo' flien'," chanted each of these apparitions; and each, after a long, slow discourse that ended more darkly than it began, retired with fatuous nods and smirks of satisfaction, leaving Rudolph dismayed by a sense of cryptic negotiation in which he had been found wanting.

Noon brought the only other interval, when two solemn "boys" stole in with curry and beer. Eat he could not in this lazaret, but sipped a little of the dark Kirin brew, and plunged again into his researches. Alone with his lamp and rustling papers, he fought through perplexities, now whispering, now silent, like a student rapt in some midnight fervor.

"What ho! Mustn't work this fashion!" Heywood's voice woke him, sudden as a gust of sharp air. "Makee finish!"

The summons was both welcome and unwelcome; for as their chairs jostled homeward through the reeking twilight, Rudolph felt the glow of work fade like the mockery of wine. The strange seizure returned,--exile, danger, incomprehensibility, settled down upon him, cold and steady as the rain. Tea, at Heywood's house, was followed by tobacco, tobacco by sherry, and this by a dinner from yesterday's game-bag. The two men said little, sitting dejected, as if by agreement. But when Heywood rose, he changed into gayety as a man slips on a jacket.

"Now, then, for the masked ball! I mean, we can't carry these long faces to the club, can we? Ladies' Night--what larks!" He caught up his cap, with a grimace. "The Lord loveth a cheerful liar. Come ahead!"

On the way, he craned from his chair to shout, in the darkness:--

"I say! If you can do a turn of any sort, let the women have it. All the fun they get. Be an ass, like the rest of us. Maskee how silly! Mind you, it's all hands, these concerts!"

No music, but the click of ivory and murmur of voices came down the stairway of the club. At first glance, as Rudolph rose above the floor, the gloomy white loft seemed vacant as ever; at second glance, embarrassingly full of Europeans. Four strangers grounded their cues long enough to shake his hand. "Mr. Nesbit,--Sturgeon--Herr Kempner--Herr Teppich,"--he bowed stiffly to each, ran the battery of their inspection, and found himself saluting three other persons at the end of the room, under a rosy, moon-bellied lantern. A gray matron, stout, and too tightly dressed for comfort, received him uneasily, a dark-eyed girl befriended him with a look and a quiet word, while a tall man, nodding a vigorous mop of silver hair, crushed his hand in a great bony fist.

"Mrs. Earle," Heywood was saying, "Miss Drake, and--how are you, padre?--Dr. Earle."

"Good-evening," boomed the giant, in a deep and musical bass. "We are very glad, very glad." His voice vibrated through the room, without effort. It struck one with singular force, like the shrewd, kind brightness of his eyes, light blue, and oddly benevolent, under brows hard as granite. "Sit down, Mr. Hackh," he ordered genially, "and give us news of the other world! I mean," he laughed, "west of Suez. Smoking's allowed--here, try that!"

He commanded them, as it were, to take their ease,--the women among cushions on a rattan couch, the men stretched in long chairs. He put questions, indolent, friendly questions, opening vistas of reply and recollection; so that Rudolph, answering, felt the first return of homely comfort. A feeble return, however, and brief: in the pauses of talk, misgiving swarmed in his mind, like the leaping vermin of last night. The world into which he had been thrown still appeared disorderly, incomprehensible, and dangerous. The plague--it still recurred in his thoughts like a sombre motive; these friendly people were still strangers; and for a moment now and then their talk, their smiles, the click of billiards, the cool, commonplace behavior, seemed a foolhardy unconcern, as of men smoking in a powder magazine.

"Clearing a bit, outside," called Nesbit. A little, wiry fellow, with cheerful Cockney speech, he stood chalking his cue at a window. "I say, what's the matter one piecee picnic this week? Pink Pagoda, eh? Mrs. Gilly 's back, you know."

"No, is she?" wheezed the fat Sturgeon, with something like enthusiasm. "Now we'll brighten up! By Jove, that's good news. That's worth hearing. Eh, Heywood?"

"Rather!" drawled Rudolph's friend, with an alacrity that seemed half cynical, half enigmatic.

A quick tread mounted the stairs, and into the room rose Dr. Chantel. He bowed gracefully to the padre's group, but halted beside the players. Whatever he said, they forgot their game, and circled the table to listen. He spoke earnestly, his hands fluttering in nervous gestures.

"Something's up," grumbled Heywood, "when the doctor forgets to pose."

Behind Chantel, as he wheeled, heaved the gray bullet-head and sturdy shoulders of Gilly.

"Alone?" called the padre. "Why, where's the Mem?"

He came up with evident weariness, but replied cheerfully:--

"She's very sorry, and sent chin-chins all round. But to-night--Her journey, you know. She's resting.--I hope we've not delayed the concert?"

"Last man starts it!" Heywood sprang up, flung open a battered piano, and dragged Chantel to the stool. "Come, Gilly, your forfeit!"

The elder man blushed, and coughed.

"Why, really," he stammered. "Really, if you wish me to!"

Heywood slid back into his chair, grinning.

"Proud as an old peacock," he whispered to Rudolph. "Peacock's voice, too."

Dr. Chantel struck a few jangling chords, and skipping adroitly over sick notes, ran a flourish. The billiard-players joined the circle, with absent, serious faces. The singer cleared his throat, took on a preternatural solemnity, and began. In a dismal, gruff voice, he proclaimed himself a miner, deep, deep down:--

"And few, I trow, of my being know,
And few that an atom care!"

His hearers applauded this gloomy sentiment, till his cheeks flushed again with honest satisfaction. But in the full sweep of a brilliant interlude, Chantel suddenly broke down.

"I cannot," he declared sharply. As he turned on the squealing stool, they saw his face white and strangely wrought. "I had meant," he said, with painful precision, "to say nothing to-night, and act as--I cannot. Judge you, what I feel."

He got uncertainly to his feet, hesitating.

"Ladies, you will not be alarmed." The four players caught his eye, and nodded. "It is well that you know. There is no danger here, more than--I am since disinfected. Monsieur Jolivet, my compatriot--You see, you understand. Yes, the plague."

For a space, the distant hum of the streets invaded the room. Then Heywood's book of music slapped the floor like a pistol-shot.

"You left him!" He bounced from his chair, raging. "You--Pêng! Where's my cap?"

Quick as he was, the dark-eyed girl stood blocking his way.

"Not you, Mr. Heywood," she said quietly. "I must go stay with him."

They confronted each other, man and woman, as if for a

combat of will. The outbreak of voices was cut short; the whole company stood, like Homeric armies, watching two champions. Chantel, however, broke the silence.

"Nobody must go." He eyed them all, gravely. "I left him, yes. He does not need any one. Personne. Very sudden. He went to the school sick this morning. Swollen axillae--the poor fool, not to know!--et puis--enfin--He is dead."

Heywood pitched his cap on the green field of the billiard-cloth.

"The poor pedagogue!" he said bitterly. "*He* was going Home."

Sudden, hot and cold, like the thrust of a knife, it struck Rudolph that he had heard the voice of this first victim,--the peevish voice which cried so weakly for a little silence, at early daylight, that very morning. A little silence: and he had received the great.

A gecko fell from the ceiling, with a tiny thump that made all start. He had struck the piano, and the strings answered with a faint, aeolian confusion. Then, as they regarded one another silently, a rustle, a flurry, sounded on the stairs. A woman stumbled into the loft, sobbing, crying something inarticulate, as she ran blindly toward them, with white face and wild eyes. She halted abruptly, swayed as though to fall, and turned, rather by instinct than by vision, to the other women.

"Bertha!" protested Gilly, with a helpless stare. "My dear!"

"I couldn't stay!" she cried. "The amah told me. Why did you ever let me come back? Oh, do something--help me!"

The face and the voice came to Rudolph like another trouble across a dream. He knew them, with a pang. This trembling, miserable heap, flung into the arms of the dark-eyed girl, was Mrs. Forrester.

"Go on," said the girl, calmly. She had drawn the woman down beside her on the rattan couch, and clasping her like a child, nodded toward the piano. "Go on, as if the doctor hadn't--hadn't stopped."

Heywood was first to obey.

"Come, Chantel, chantez! Here's your song." He took the stool in leap-frog fashion, and struck a droll simultaneous discord. "Come on.--Well, then, catch me on the chorus!

"Pour qu' j' finisse
Mon service
Au Tonkin je suis parti!"

To a discreet set of verses, he rattled a bravado accompaniment. Presently Chantel moved to his side, and, with the same spirit, swung into the chorus. The tumbled white figure on the couch clung to her refuge, her bright hair shining below the girl's quiet, thoughtful face. She was shaken with convulsive regularity.

In his riot of emotions, Rudolph found an over-mastering shame. A picture returned,--the Strait of Malacca, this woman in the blue moonlight, a Mistress of Life, rejoicing, alluring,--who was now the single coward in the room. But was she? The question was quick and revolting. As quickly, a choice of sides was forced on him. He understood these people, recalled Heywood's saying, and with that, some story of a regiment which lay waiting in the open, and sang while the bullets picked and chose. All together: as now these half-dozen men were roaring cheerfully:--

"Ma Tonkikí, ma Tonkikí, ma Tonkinoise,
Yen a d'autr's qui m' font les doux yeux,
Mais c'est ell' que j'aim' le mieux!"

The new recruit joined them, awkwardly.

CHAPTER IV

THE SWORD-PEN

"Wutzler was missing last night," said Heywood, lazily. He had finished breakfast, and lighted a short, fat, glossy pipe. "Just occurred to me. We must have a look in on him. Poor old Wutz, he's getting worse and worse. Chantel's right, I fancy: it's the native wife." He rose, with a short laugh. "Queer. The rest never feel so,--Nesbit, and Sturgeon, and that lot. But then, they don't fall so low as to marry theirs."

"By the way," he sneered, on the landing, "until this scare blows over, you'd better postpone any such establishment, if you intend--"

"I do not," stammered Rudolph.

To his amazement, the other clapped him on the shoulder.

"I say!" The sallow face and cynical gray eyes lighted, for the first time, with something like enthusiasm. Next moment they had darkened again, but not before he had said gruffly, "You're not a bad little chap."

Morosely, as if ashamed of this outburst, he led the way through the bare, sunny compound, and when the gate had closed rattling behind them, stated their plans concisely and sourly. "No work to-day, not a stroke! We'll just make it a holiday, catchee good time.--What? No. Rot! I won't work, and you can't. That's all there is about that. Don't be an ass! Come along. We'll go out first and see Captain Kneebone." And when Rudolph, faithful to certain tradesmen snoring in Bremen, would have protested mildly, he let fly a stinging retort, and did not regain his temper until they had passed the outskirts of the village. Yet even the quarrel seemed part of some better understanding, some new, subtle bond between two lonely men.

Before them opened a broad field dotted with curious white disks, like bone buttons thrown on a green carpet. Near at hand, coolies trotted and stooped, laying out more of these circular baskets, filled with tiny dough-balls. Makers of rice-wine, said Heywood; as he strode along explaining, he threw off his surly fit. The brilliant sunlight, the breeze stirring toward them from a background of drooping bamboos, the gabble of coolies, the faint aroma of the fermenting *no-me* cakes, began, after all, to give a truant sense of holiday.

Almost gayly, the companions threaded a marshy path to the river, and bargained with a shrewd, plump woman who squatted in the bow of a sampan. She chaffered angrily, then laughed at some unknown saying of Heywood's, and let them come aboard. Summoned by voluble scolding, her husband appeared, and placidly labored at the creaking sweep. They slipped down a river of bronze, between the oozy banks; and the war-junks, the naked fisherman, the green-coated ruins of forts, drifted past like things in reverie, while the men lay smoking, basking in bright weather. They looked up into serene spaces, and forgot the umbra of pestilence.

Heywood, now lazy, now animated, exchanged barbaric words with the boat-woman. As their tones rose and fell, she laughed. Long afterward, Rudolph was to remember her, a wholesome, capable figure in faded blue, darting keen glances from her beady eyes, flashing her white teeth in a smile, or laughing till the green pendants of false jade trembled in her ears.

"Her name is Mrs. Wu," said Heywood, between smoke-rings, "and she is a lady of humor. We are discussing the latest lawsuit, which she describes as suing a flea and winning the bite. Her maiden name was the Pretty Lily. She is captain of this sampan, and fears that her husband does not rate A. B."

Where the river disembogued, the Pretty Lily, cursing and shrilling, pattering barefoot about her craft, set a matting sail and caught the breeze. Over the copper surface of the roadstead, the sampan drew out handily. Ahead, a black, disreputable little steamer lay anchored, her name--two enormous hieroglyphics painted amidships--staring a bilious yellow in the morning sun. Under these, at last, the sampan came bumping, unperceived or neglected.

Overhead, a pair of white shoes protruded from the rail in a blue film of smoke. They twitched, as a dry cackle of laughter broke out.

"Kut Sing, ahoy!" shouted Heywood. "On deck! Kneebone!"

The shoes whipped inboard. Outboard popped a ruddy little face, set in the green circle of a *topi*, and contorted with laughter.

"Listen to this, will ye!" cried the apparition, as though illustrating a point. Leaning his white sleeves on the rail, cigar in one fist, Tauchnitz volume in the other, he roared down over the side a passage of prose, from which his visitors caught only the words "Ginger Dick" and "Peter Russet," before mirth strangled him.

"God bless a man," he cried, choking, "that can make a lonesome old beggar laugh, out here! Eh, what? How he ever thinks up--But he's took to writing plays, they tell me. Plays!" He scowled ferociously. "Fat lot o' good they are, for skippers, and planters, and gory exiles! Eh, what? Be-george, I'll write him a chit! *I'll* tell him! Plays be damned; we want more stories!"

Red and savage, he hurled the book fluttering into the sea, then swore in consternation.

"Oh, I say!" he wailed. "Fish her out! I've not finished her. My intention was, ye know, to fling the bloomin' cigar!"

Heywood, laughing, rescued the volume on a long bamboo.

"Just came out on the look-see, captain," he called up. "Can't board you. Plague ashore."

"Plague be 'anged!" scoffed the little captain. "That hole's no worse with plague than't is without. Got two cases on board, myself--coolies. Stowed 'em topside, under the boats.--Come up here, ye castaway! Come up, ye goatskin Robinson Crusoe, and get a white man's chow!"

He received them on deck,--a red, peppery little officer, whose shaven cheeks and close gray hair gave him the look of a parson gone wrong, a hedge-priest run away to sea. Two tall Chinese boys scurried about with wicker chairs, with trays of bottles, ice, and cheroots, while he barked his orders, like a fox-terrier commanding a pair of solemn dock-rats. The white men soon lounged beside the wheel-house.

"So you brought Mrs. Forrester," drawled Heywood.

Rudolph, wondering if they saw him wince, listened with painful eagerness. But the captain disposed of that subject very simply.

"*She's* no good." He stared up at the grimy awning. "What I'm thinking is, will that there Dacca babu at Koprah slip me through his blessed quarantine for twenty-five dollars. What?"

Their talk drifted far away from Rudolph, far from China itself, to touch a hundred ports and islands, Cebu and Sourabaya, Tavoy and Selangor. They talked of men and women, a death at Zamboanga, a birth at Chittagong, of obscure heroism or suicide, and fortunes made or lost; while the two boys, gentle, melancholy, gliding silent in bright blue robes, spread a white tablecloth, clamped it with shining brass, and laid the tiffin. Then the talk flowed on, the feast made a tiny clatter of jollity in the slumbering noon, in the silence of an ocean and a continent. And when at last the visitors clambered down the iron side, they went victorious with Spanish wine.

"Mind ye," shouted Captain Kneebone, from the rail, "that don't half exhaust the subjeck o' lott'ries! Why, luck"--He shook both fists aloft, triumphantly, as if they had been full of money. "Just ye wait. I've a tip from Calcutta that--Never mind. Bar sells, when that fortch'n comes, my boy, the half's yours! Home we go, remember that!"

The sampan drew away. Sweeping his arm violently, to threaten the coast of China and the whole range of his vision,--

"You're the one man," he roared, "that makes all this mess-- worth a cowrie!"

Heywood laughed, waved his helmet, and when at last he turned, sat looking downward with a queer smile.

"Illusions!" he chuckled. "What would a chap ever do without 'em? Old Kneebone there: his was always that--a fortune in a lottery, and then Home! Illusions! And he's no fool, either. Good navigator. Decent old beggar." He waved his helmet again, before stretching out to sleep. "Do you know, I believe--he *would* take me."

The clinkered hills, quivering in the west, sank gradually into the heated blur above the plains. As gradually, the two men sank into dreams.

Furious, metallic cries from the Pretty Lily woke them, in the blue twilight. She had moored her sampan alongside a flight of stone steps, up which, vigorously, with a bamboo, she now prodded her husband. He contended, snarling, but mounted; and when Heywood's silver fell jingling into her palm, lighted his lantern and scuffed along, a churlish guide. At the head of the slimy stairs, Heywood rattled a ponderous gate in a wall, and shouted. Some one came running, shot bolts, and swung the door inward. The lantern showed the tawny, grinning face of a servant, as they passed into a small garden, of dwarf orange trees pent in by a lofty, whitewashed wall.

"These grounds are yours, Hackh," said Heywood. "Your predecessor's boy; and there"--pointing to a lonely barrack that loomed white over the stunted grove--"there's your house. You draw the largest in the station. A Portuguese nunnery, it was, built years ago. My boys are helping set it to rights; but if you don't mind, I'd like you to stay on at my beastly hut until this--this business takes a turn. Plenty of time." He nodded at the fat little orange trees. "We may live to take our chow under those yet, of an evening. Also a drink. Eh?"

The lantern skipped before them across the garden, through a penitential courtyard, and under a vaulted way to the main door and the road. With Rudolph, the obscure garden and echoing house left a sense of magical ownership, sudden and fleeting, like riches in the Arabian Nights. The road, leaving on the right a low hill, or convex field, that heaved against the lower stars, now led the wanderers down a lane of hovels, among dim squares of smoky lamplight.

Wu, their lantern-bearer, had turned back, and they had begun to pass a few quiet, expectant shops, when a screaming voice, ahead, outraged the evening stillness.

At the first words, Heywood doubled his pace.

"Come along. Here's a lark--or a tragedy."

Jostling through a malodorous crowd that blockaded the quarrel, they gained the threshold of a lighted shop. Against a rank of orderly shelves, a fat merchant stood at bay, silent, quick-eyed, apprehensive. Before him, like an actor in a mad scene, a sobbing ruffian, naked to the waist, convulsed with passion, brandished wild fists and ranted with incredible sounds. When breath failed, he staggered, gasping, and swept his audience with the glazed, unmeaning stare of drink or lunacy. The merchant spoke up, timid and deprecating. As though the words were vitriol, the other started, whirled face to face, and was seized with a new raving.

Something protruded at his waistband, like a rudimentary, Darwinian stump. To this, all at once, his hand flung back. With a wrench and a glitter, he flourished a blade above his head. Heywood sprang to intervene, in the same instant that the disturber of trade swept his arm down in frenzy. Against his own body, hilt and fist thumped home, with the sound as of a football lightly punted. He turned, with a freezing look of surprise, plucked at the haft, made one step calmly and tentatively toward the door, stumbled, and lay retching and coughing.

The fat shop-keeper wailed like a man beside himself. He gabbled, imploring Heywood. The young man nodded. "Yes, yes," he repeated irritably, staring down at the body, but listening to the stream of words.

Murmurs had risen, among the goblin faces blinking in the doorway. Behind them, a sudden voice called out two words which were caught up and echoed harshly in the street. Heywood whipped about.

"Never called me that before," he said quickly. "Come outside."

He flung back a hurried sentence to the merchant, caught Rudolph's arm, and plunged into the crowd. The yellow men gave passage mechanically, but with lowering faces. Once free in the muddy path, he halted quickly, and looked about.

"Might have known," he grumbled. "Never called me 'Foreign Dog' before, or 'Jesus man,' He set 'em on."

Rudolph followed his look. In the dim light, at the outskirts of the rabble, a man was turning away, with an air of contempt or unconcern. The long, pale, oval face, the hard eyes gleaming with thought, had vanished at a glance. A tall, slight figure, stooping in his long robe, he glided into the darkness. For all his haste, the gait was not the gait of a coolie.

"That," said Heywood, turning into their former path, "that was Fang, the Sword-Pen, so-called. Very clever chap. Of the two most dangerous men in the district, he's one." They had swung along briskly for several minutes, before he added: "The other most dangerous man--you've met him already. If I'm not mistaken, he's no less a person than the Reverend James Earle."

"What!" exclaimed Rudolph, in dull bewilderment.

"Yes," grunted his friend. "The padre. We must find him to-night, and report."

He strode forward, with no more comment. At his side, Rudolph moved as a soldier, carried onward by pressure and automatic rhythm, moves in the apathy of a forced march. The day had been so real, so wholesome, full of careless talk and of sunlight. And now this senseless picture blotted all else, and remained,--each outline sharper in memory, the smoky lamp brighter, the blow of the hilt louder, the smell of peanut oil more pungent. The episode, to him, was a disconnected, unnecessary fragment, one bloody strand in the whole terrifying snarl. But his companion stalked on in silence, like a man who saw a pattern in the web of things, and was not pleased.

CHAPTER V

IN TOWN

Night, in that maze of alleys, was but a more sinister day. The same slant-eyed men, in broken files, went scuffing over filthy stone, like wanderers lost in a tunnel. The same inexplicable noises endured, the same smells. Under lamps, the shaven foreheads still bent toward microscopic labor. The curtained window of a fantan shop still glowed in orange translucency, and from behind it came the murmur and the endless chinking of cash, where Fortune, a bedraggled, trade-fallen goddess, split hairs with coolies for poverty or zero. Nothing was altered in these teeming galleries, except that turbid daylight had imperceptibly given place to this other dimness, in which lanterns swung like tethered fire-balloons. Life went on, mysteriously, without change or sleep.

While the two white men shouldered their way along, a strange chorus broke out, as though from among the crowded carcasses in a butcher's stall. Shrill voices rose in unearthly discord, but the rhythm was not of Asia.

"There goes the hymn!" scoffed Heywood. He halted where, between the butcher's and a book-shop, the song poured loud through an open doorway. Nodding at a placard, he added: "Here we are: 'Jesus Religion Chapel.' Hear 'em yanging! 'There is a gate that stands ajar.' That being the case, in you go!"

Entering a long, narrow room, lighted from sconces at either side, they sat down together, like schoolmates, on a low form near the door. From a dais across at the further end, the vigorous white head of Dr. Earle dominated the company,--a strange company, of lounging Chinamen who sucked at enormous bamboo pipes, or squinted aimlessly at the vertical inscriptions on the walls, or wriggling about, stared at the late-comers, nudged their neighbors, and pointed, with guttural exclamations. The song had ended, and the padre was lifting up his giant's voice. To Rudolph, the words had been mere sound and fury, but for a compelling honesty that needed no translation. This man was not preaching to heathen, but talking to men. His eyes had the look of one who speaks earnestly of matters close at hand, direct, and simple. Along the forms, another and another man forgot to plait his queue, or squirm, or suck laboriously at his pipe. They listened, stupid or intent. When some waif from the outer labyrinth scuffed in, affable, impudent, hailing his friends across the room, he made but a ripple of unrest, and sank gaping among the others like a fish in a pool.

Even Heywood sat listening--with more attention than respect, for once he muttered, "Rot!" Toward the close, however, he leaned across and whispered, "The old boy reels it off rather well to-night. Different to what one imagined."

Rudolph, for his part, sat watching and listening, surprised by a new and curious thought.

A band of huddled converts sang once more, in squealing discords, with an air of sad, compulsory, and diabolic sarcasm. A few "inquirers" slouched forward, and surrounding the tall preacher, questioned him concerning the new faith. The last, a broad, misshapen fellow with hanging jowls, was answered sharply. He stood arguing, received another snub, and went out bawling and threatening, with the contorted face and clumsy flourishes of some fabulous hero on a screen.

The missionary approached smiling, but like a man who has finished the day's work.

"That fellow--Good-evening: and welcome to our Street Chapel, Mr. Hackh--That fellow," he glanced after the retreating figure, "he's a lesson in perseverance, gentlemen. A merchant, well-to-do: he has a lawsuit coming on-- notorious--and tries to join us for protection. Cheaper to buy a little belief, you know, than to pay Yamên fines. Every night he turns up, grinning and bland. I tell him it won't do, and out he goes, snorting like a dragon."

Rudolph's impulse came to a head.

"Dr. Earle," he stammered, "I owe you a gratitude. You spoke to these people so--as--I do not know. But I listened,

I felt--Before always are they devils, images! And after I hear you, they are as men."

The other shook his great head like a silver mane, and laughed.

"My dear young man," he replied, "they're remarkably like you and me."

After a pause, he added soberly:--

"Images? Yes, you're right, sir. So was Adam. The same clay, the same image." His deep voice altered, his eyes lighted shrewdly, as he turned to Heywood. "This is an unexpected pleasure."

"Quite," said the young man, readily. "If you don't mind, padre, you made Number One talk. Fast bowling, and no wides. But we really came for something else." In a few brief sentences, he pictured the death in the shop.--So, like winking! The beggar gave himself the iron, fell down, and made finish. Now what I pieced out, from his own bukhing, and the merchant's, was this:--

"The dead man was one Aú-yöng, a cormorant-fisher. Some of his best birds died, he had a long run of bad luck, and came near starving. So he contrived, rather cleverly, to steal about a hundred catties of Fuh-kien hemp. The owner, this merchant, went to the elders of Aú-yöng's neighborhood, who found and restored the hemp, nearly all. Merchant lets the matter drop. But the neighbors kept after this cormorant fellow, worked one beastly squeeze or another, ingenious baiting, devilish--Rot! you know their neighborhoods better than I! Well, they pushed him down-hill--poor devil, showing that's always possible, no bottom! He brooded, and all that, till he thought the merchant and the Jesus religion were the cause of all. So bang he goes down the pole,-- gloriously drunk,--marches into his enemy's shop, and uses that knife. The joke is now on the merchant, eh?"

"Just a moment," begged the padre. "One thread I don't follow--the religion. Who was Christian? The merchant?"

"Well, rather! Thought I told you," said Heywood. "One of yours--big, mild chap--Chok Chung."

The elder man sat musing.

"Yes," the deep bass rumbled in the empty chapel, "he's one of us. Extremely honest. I'm--I'm very sorry. There may be trouble."

"Must be, sir," prompted the younger. "The mob, meanwhile, just stood there, dumb,--mutes and audience, you know. All at once, the hindmost began squalling 'Foreign Dog,' 'Goat Man.' We stepped outside, and there, passing, if you like, was that gentle bookworm, Mr. Fang."

"Fang?" echoed the padre, as in doubt. "I've heard the name."

"Heard? Why, doctor," cried Heywood, "that long, pale chap,--lives over toward the Dragon Spring. Confucian, very strict; keen reader; might be a mandarin, but prefers the country gentleman sort; bally mischief-maker, he's done more people in the eye than all the Yamên hacks and all their false witnesses together! Hence his nickname--the Sword-Pen."

Dr. Earle sharpened his heavy brows, and studied the floor.

"Fang, the Sword-Pen," he growled; "yes, there will be trouble. He hates us. Given this chance--Humph! Saul of Tarsus.--We're not the Roman Church," he added, with his first trace of irritation. "Always occurring, this thing."

Once more he meditated; then heaved his big shoulders to let slip the whole burden.

"One day at a time," he laughed. "Thank you for telling us.-- You see, Mr. Hackh, they're not devils. The only fault is, they're just human beings. You don't speak the language? I'll send you my old teacher."

They talked of things indifferent; and when the young men were stumbling along the streets, he called after them a resounding "Good-night! Thanks!"--and stood a resolute, gigantic silhouette, filling, as a right Doone filled their doorframe, the entrance to his deserted chapel.

At his gate, felt Rudolph, they had unloaded some weight of responsibility. He had not only accepted it, but lightened them further, girt them, by a word and a look. Somehow, for the first time since landing, Rudolph perceived that through this difficult, troubled, ignorant present, a man might burrow toward a future gleam. The feeling was but momentary. As for Heywood, he still marched on grimly, threading the stuffed corridors like a man with a purpose.

"No dinner!" he snapped. "Catchee bymby, though. We must see Wutzler first. To lose sight of any man for twenty-four hours, nowadays,--Well, it's not hardly fair. Is it?"

They turned down a black lane, carpeted with dry rubbish. At long intervals, a lantern guttering above a door showed them a hand's-breadth of the dirty path, a litter of broken withes and basket-weavers' refuse, between the mouldy wall of the town and a row of huts, no less black and silent. In this greasy rift the air lay thick, as though smeared into a groove.

Suddenly, among the hovels, they groped along a checkered surface of brick-work. The flare of Heywood's match revealed a heavy wooden door, which he hammered with his fist. After a time, a disgruntled voice within snarled something in the vernacular. Heywood laughed.

"Ai-yah! Who's afraid? Wutzler, you old pirate, open up!"

A bar clattered down, the door swung back, and there, raising a glow-worm lantern of oiled paper, stood such a timorous little figure as might have ventured out from a masquerade of gnomes. The wrinkled face was Wutzler's, but his weazened body was lost in the glossy black folds of a native jacket, and below the patched trousers, his bare ankles and coolie-sandals of straw moved uneasily, as though trying to hide behind each other.

"Kom in," said this hybrid, with a nervous cackle. "I thought you are thiefs. Kom in."

Following through a toy courtyard, among shadow hints of pigmy shrubs and rockery, they found themselves cramped in a bare, clean cell, lighted by a European lamp, but smelling of soy and Asiatics. Stiff black-wood chairs lined the walls. A distorted landscape on rice-paper, narrow scarlet panels inscribed with black cursive characters, pith flowers from Amoy, made blots of brightness.

"It iss not moch, gentlemen," sighed Wutzler, cringing. "But I am ver' glad."

Heywood flung himself into a chair.

"Not dead yet, you rascal?" he cried. "And we came all the way to see you. No chow, either."

"Oh, allow me," mumbled their host, in a flutter. "My--she-- I will speak, I go bring you." He shuffled away, into some further chamber.

Heywood leaned forward quickly.

"Eat it," he whispered, "whether you can or not! Pleases the old one, no bounds. We're his only visitors--"

"Here iss not moch whiskey." Wutzler came shambling in, held a bottle against the light, and squinted ruefully at the yellow dregs. "I will gif you a *kong* full, but I haf not."

He dodged out again. They heard his angry whispers, and a small commotion of the household,--brazen dishes clinking, squeals, titters, and tiny bare feet skipping about,--all the flurry of a rabbit-hutch in Wonderland. Once, near the threshold, a chubby face, very pale, with round eyes of shining jet, peered cautious as a mouse, and popped out of sight with a squeak. Wutzler, red with excitement, came and went like an anxious waiter, bringing in the feast.

"Here iss not moch," he repeated sadly. But there were bits of pig-skin stewed in oil; bean-cakes; steaming buns of wheat-flour, stuffed with dice of fat pork and lumps of sugar; three-cornered rice puddings, *no-me* boiled in plantain-leaf wrappers; with the last of the whiskey, in green cups. While the two men ate, the shriveled outcast beamed timidly, hovering about them, fidgeting.

"Herr Hackh," he suddenly exclaimed, in a queer, strained voice, "you do not know how dis yong man iss goot! No! He hass to me--*immer*--" He choked, turned away, and began fussing with the pith flowers; but not before Rudolph had seen a line glistening down the sun-dried cheeks.

"Stuff! Cadging for chow, does one acquire merit?" retorted Heywood, over his shoulder. "You talk like a bonze, Wutz." He winked. "I'd rather hear the sing-song box."

"*Ach so*, I forget!" Still whimpering, Wutzler dragged something from a corner, squatted, and jerked at a crank, with a noise of ratchets. "She blay not so moch now," he snuffled. "Captain Kneepone he has gifen her, when she iss all op inside for him. I haf rebaired, but she blay only one song yet. A man does not know, Herr Hackh, what he may be. Once I haf piano, and viola my own, yes, and now haf I diss small, laffing, sick teufel!" He rose, and faced Heywood with a trembling, passionate gesture. "But diss yong man, he stand by der oldt fellow!" The streaming eyes blinked absurdly.

Behind him, with a whirring sound, a metallic voice assailed them in a gabble of words, at first husky and broken, then clear, nasal, a voice from neither Europe nor Asia, but America:--

"Then did I laff?
Ooh, aha-ha ha ha,
Ha, ha, ha, ha, ha!
I could not help but laffing,
Ooh, aha-ha ..."

From a throat of tin, it mocked them insanely with squealing, black-hearted guffaws. Heywood sat smoking, with the countenance of a stoic; but when the laughter in the box was silent, he started abruptly.

"We're off, old chap," he announced. "Bedtime. Just came to see you were all up-standing. Tough as ever? Good! Don't let--er--anything carry you off."

At the gate, Wutzler held aloft his glow-worm lantern.

"Dose fellows catch me?" he mumbled, "Der plagues--dey will forget me. All zo many shoots, *kugel*, der bullet,--'*gilt's mir, oder gilt es dir?*' Men are dead in der Silk-Weafer Street. Dey haf hong up nets, and dorns, to keep out der plague's-goblins off deir house. Listen, now, dey beat gongs!--But we are white men. You--you tell me zo, to-night!" He blubbered something incoherent, but as the gate slammed they heard the name of God, in a broken benediction.

They had groped out of the cleft, and into a main corridor, before Heywood paused.

"That devil in the box!" He shook himself like a spaniel. "Queer it should get into me so. But I hate being laughed at by--anybody."

A confused thunder of gongs, the clash of cymbals smothered in the distance, maintained a throbbing uproar, pierced now and then by savage yells, prolonged and melancholy. As the two wanderers listened,--

"Where's the comfort," said Heywood, gloomily, "of knowing somebody's worse off?--No, I wasn't thinking of Wutzler, then. Talk of germs! why, over there, it's goblins they're scaring away. Think, behind their nets and thorns, what wretches--women, too, and kids--may be crouched down, quaking, sick with terror. Humph!--I don't mind saying"--for a moment his hand lay on Rudolph's shoulder-- "that I loathe giving this muck-hole the satisfaction--I'd hate to go Out here, that's all."

CHAPTER VI

THE PAGODA

He was spared that inconvenience. The untimely rain and cold, some persons said, the few days of untimely heat following, had drowned or dried, frozen or burnt out, the seeds of peril. But accounts varied, reasons were plentiful. Soldiers had come down from the chow city, two-score *li* inland, and charging through the streets, hacking and slashing the infested air, had driven the goblins over the walls, with a great shout of victory. A priest had freighted a kite with all the evil, then cut it adrift in the sky. A mob had dethroned the God of Sickness, and banished his effigy in a paper junk, launched on the river at night, in flame. A geomancer proclaimed that a bamboo grove behind the town formed an angle most correct, germane, and pleasant to the Azure Dragon and the White Tiger, whose occult currents, male and female, run throughout Nature. For any or all of these reasons, the town was delivered. The pestilence vanished, as though it had come but to grant Monsieur Jolivet his silence, and to add a few score uncounted living wretches to the dark, mighty, imponderable host of ancestors.

The relief, after dragging days of uncertainty, came to Rudolph like a sea-breeze to a stoker. To escape and survive,--the bare experience seemed to him at first an act of merit, the deed of a veteran. The interim had been packed with incongruity. There had been a dinner with Kempner, solemn, full of patriotism and philosophy; a drunken dinner at Teppich's; another, and a worse, at Nesbit's; and the banquet of a native merchant, which began at four o'clock on melon-seeds, tea, black yearling eggs, and a hot towel, and ended at three in the morning on rice-brandy and betel served by unreal women with chalked faces and vermilion-spotted lips, simpering and melancholy. By day, there was work, or now and then a lesson with Dr. Earle's teacher, a little aged Chinaman of intricate, refined, and plaintive courtesy. Under his guidance Rudolph learned rapidly, taking to study as a prodigal might take to drink. And with increasing knowledge came increasing tranquillity; as when he found that the hideous cry, startling him at every dawn, was the signal not for massacre, but buffalo-milk.

Then, too, came the mild excitement of moving into his own house, the Portuguese nunnery. Through its desolate, lime-coated spaces, his meagre belongings were scattered all too easily; but the new servants, their words and ways, not only kept his hands full, but gave strange food for thought. The silent evenings, timed by the plash of a frog in a pool, a cry from the river, or the sing-song of a "boy" improvising some endless ballad below-stairs; drowsy noons above the little courtyard, bare and peaceful as a jail; homesick moments at the window, when beyond the stunted orangery, at sunset, the river was struck amazingly from bronze to indigo, or at dawn flashed from pearl-gray to flowing brass;--all these, and nights between sleep and waking, when fancy peopled the echoing chambers with the visionary lives, now ended, of meek, brown sisters from Goa or Macao, gave to Rudolph intimations, vague, profound, and gravely happy, as of some former existence almost recaptured. Once more he felt himself a householder in the Arabian tales.

And yet, when his life was growing all but placid, across it shot some tremor of disquieting knowledge.

One evening, after a busy day among his piece-goods, he had walked afield with Heywood, and back by an aimless circuit through the twilight. His companion had been taciturn, of late; and they halted, without speaking, where a wide pool gleamed toward a black, fantastic belt of knotted willows and sharp-curving roofs. Through these broke the shadow of a small pagoda, jagged as a war-club of shark's teeth. Vesper cymbals clashed faintly in a temple, and from its open door the first plummet of lamplight began to fathom the dark margin. A short bridge curved high, like a camel's hump, over the glimmering half-circle of a single arch. Close by, under a drooping foreground of branches, a stake upheld an oblong placard of neat symbols, like a cartouche to explain a painting.

"It is very beautiful," ventured Rudolph, twisting up his blond moustache with satisfaction. "Very sightly. I would say--picturesque, no?"

"Very," said Heywood, absently. "Willow Pattern."

"And the placard, so finishing, so artistic--That says?"

"Eh, what? Oh, I wasn't listening." Heywood glanced carelessly at the upright sentence. That's a notice:--

"'Girls May Not be Drowned in This Pond.'"

He started on, without comment. Without reply, Rudolph followed, gathering as he walked the force of this tremendous hint. Slow, far-reaching, it poisoned the elegiac beauty of the scene, alienated the night, and gave to the fading country-side a yet more ancient look, sombre and implacable. He was still pondering this, when across their winding foot-path, with a quick thud of hoofs, swept a pair of equestrian silhouettes. It was half glimpse, half conjecture,--the tough little ponies trotting stubbornly, a rider who leaned across laughing, and a woman who gayly cried at him: "You really do understand me, don't you?" The two jogging shadows melted in the bamboo tracery, like things blown down the wind. But for years Rudolph had known the words, the laugh, the beguiling cadence, and could have told what poise of the head went with them, what dangerous glancing light. Suddenly, without reason, he felt a gust of rage. It was he that understood. It was to him these things belonged. The memory of her weakness was lost in the shining memory of her power. He should be riding there, in the dusk of this lonely and cruel land.

Heywood had thrown after them a single gloomy stare, down the pointed aisle of bamboos.

"Well matched!" he growled. "Chantel--He bounds in the saddle, and he bounds afoot!"

Rudolph knew that he had hated Chantel at sight.

He could not bring himself, next day, to join their party for tiffin at the Flowery Pagoda. But in the midst of his brooding, Teppich and the fat Sturgeon assailed the nunnery gate with pot-valiant blows and shouts. They had brought chairs, to carry him off; and being in no mood to fail, though panting and struggling, they packed him into a palanquin with many bottles of the best wine known to Fliegelman and Sons. By a short cut through the streets-- where checkered sunshine, through the lattice roof, gave a muddy, subdued light as in a roiled aquarium--the revelers passed the inland wall. Here, in the shade, grooms awaited them with ponies; and scrambling into saddle, they trotted off through gaps in the bamboos, across a softly rolling country. Tortuous foot-paths of vivid pink wound over brilliant green terraces of young paddy. The pink crescents of new graves scarred the hillsides, already scalloped and crinkled with shelving abodes of the venerable dead. Great hats of farmers stooping in the fields, gleamed in the sun like shields of brass. Over knolls and through hollows the little cavalcade jogged steadily, till, mounting a gentle eminence, they wound through a grove of camphor and Flame-of-the-Forest. Above the branches rose the faded lilac shaft of an ancient pagoda, ruinously adorned with young trees and wild shrubs clinging in the cornices.

At the foot of this aged fantasy in stone, people were laughing. The three riders broke cover in time to see Mrs. Forrester, flushed and radiant, end some narrative with a droll pantomime. She stood laughing, the life and centre of a delighted group.

"And Gilbert Forrester," she cried, turning archly on her husband, "said that wasn't funny!"

Gilly tugged his gray moustache, in high good-nature. Chantel, Nesbit, and Kempner laughed uproariously, the padre and the dark-eyed Miss Drake quietly, Heywood more quietly, while even stout, uneasy Mrs. Earle smiled as in duty bound. A squad of Chinese boys, busy with tiffin-baskets, found time to grin. To this lively actress in the white gown they formed a sylvan audience under the gnarled boughs and the pagoda.

"Too late!" called the white-haired giant, indulgently, to the dismounting trio. "Mr. Hackh, you should have come spurring."

Rudolph advanced, pale, but with a calmness of which, afterward, he was justly proud. The heroine of the moment turned toward him quickly, with a look more natural, more sincere, than she had ever given him.

"Is this Mr. Hackh?" she said graciously. "I've heard so much about you!"

The young man himself was almost deceived. Was there a German mail-boat? Was there a club, from which he had stolen out while she wept, ignominiously, in that girl's arms? And then of a sudden he perceived, with a fatuous pleasure, how well she knew him, to know that he had never spoken. His English, as he drew up a stool beside Miss Drake, was wild and ragged; but he found her an astonishing refuge. For the first time, he recalled that this quiet girl had been beautiful, the other night; and though now by day that beauty was rather of line than of color, he could not understand how it had been overlooked. Tiffin, meanwhile, sped by like an orgy. He remembered asking so many questions, about the mission hospital and her school for orphans, that the girl began at last to answer with constraint, and with puzzled, sidelong scrutiny. He remembered how even the tolerant Heywood shot a questioning glance toward his wine-glass. He remembered telling a brilliant story, and reciting "Old Captain Mau in Vegesack,"--rhymes long forgotten, now fluent and spontaneous. The applause was a triumph. Through it, as through a haze, he saw a pair of wide blue eyes shining with startled admiration.

But the best came when the sun had lowered behind the grove, the company grown more silent, and Mrs. Forrester, leaning beside the door of the tower, turned the great pegs of a Chinese lute. The notes tinkled like a mandolin, but with now and then an alien wail, a lament unknown to the West. "Sing for us," begged the dark-eyed girl; "a native song." The other smiled, and bending forward as if to recollect, began in a low voice, somewhat veiled, but musical and full of meaning. "The Jasmine Flower," first; then, "My Love is Gathering Dolichos"; and then she sang the long Ballad of the Rice,--of the husband and wife planting side by side, the springing of the green blades, the harvest by millions upon millions of sheaves, the wealth of the State, more fragrant to ancestors than offerings of spice:--

"...O Labor and Love and hallowed Land!
Think you these things are but still to come?
Think you they are but near at hand,
Only now and here?--Behold.
They were the same in years of old!"

In her plaintive interlude, the slant-eyed servants watched

her, nodding and muttering under the camphor trees.

"And here's a song of exile," she said. "I render it very badly."--Rudolph had never seen her face like this, bending intently above the lute. It was as though in the music she found and disclosed herself, without guile.

"...Blue was the sky,
And blue the rice-pool water lay
Holding the sky;
Blue was the robe she wore that day.
Alas, my sorrow! Why
Must life bear all away,
Away, away,
Ah, my beloved, why?"

A murmur of praise went round the group, as she put aside the instrument.

"The sun's getting low," she said lightly, "and I *must* see that view from the top." Chantel was rising, but sat down again with a scowl, as she turned to Rudolph. "You've never seen it, Mr. Hackh? Do come help me up."

Inside, with echoing steps, they mounted in a squalid well, obscurely lighted from the upper windows, toward which decaying stairs rose in a dangerous spiral, without guard-rail. A misstep being no trifle, Rudolph offered his hand for the mere safety; but she took it with a curious little laugh. They climbed cautiously. Once, at a halt, she stood very close, with eyes shining large in the dusk. Her slight body trembled, her head shook with stifled merriment, like a girl overcome by mischief.

"What a queer little world!" she whispered. "You and I here!--I never dreamed you could be funny. It made me so proud of you, down there!"

He muttered something vague; and--the stairs ending in ruin at the fourth story--handed her carefully through the window to a small outer balustrade. As they stood together at the rail, he knew not whether to be angry, suspicious, or glad.

"I love this prospect," she began quietly. "That's why I wanted you to come."

Beyond the camphors, a wide, strange landscape glowed in the full, low-streaming light. The ocean lay a sapphire band in the east; in the west, on a long ridge, undulated the gray battlements of a city, the antique walls, warmed and glorified, breasting the flood of sunset. All between lay vernal fields and hillocks, maidenhair sprays of bamboo, and a wandering pattern of pink foot-paths. Slowly along one of these, a bright-gowned merchant rode a white pony, his bells tinkling in the stillness of sea and land. Everywhere, like other bells more tiny and shrill, sounded the trilling of frogs.

As the two on the pagoda stood listening,--

"It was before Rome," she declared thoughtfully. "Before Egypt, and has never changed. You and I are just--" She broke off, humming:--

"Only here and now? Behold
They were the same in years of old!"

Her mood colored the scene: the aged continuity of life oppressed him. Yet he chose rather to watch the straggling battlements, far off, than to meet her eyes or see her hair gleaming in the sun. Through many troubled days he had forgotten her, despised her, bound his heart in triple brass against a future in her hateful neighborhood; and now, beside her at this time-worn rail, he was in danger of being happy. It was inglorious. He tried to frown.

"You poor boy." Suddenly, with an impulse that must have been generous, she rested her hand on his arm. "I was sorry. I thought of you so often."

At these close quarters, her tremulous voice and searching upward glance meant that she alone understood all his troubles. He started, turned for some rush of overwhelming speech, when a head popped through the window behind them.

"Boot and saddle, Mrs. Forrester," announced Heywood. His lean young face was very droll and knowing. "We're leaving, bottom-side."

"Thank you so much, Maurice," she answered, perhaps dryly. "You're a dear, to climb all those dreadful stairs."

"Oh!" said Heywood, with his gray eyes fastened on Rudolph, "no trouble."

All three went down the dark well together.

When the company were mounted, and trooping downhill through the camphor shadow, Heywood's pony came sidling against Rudolph's, till legging chafed legging.

"You blossomed, old boy," he whispered. "Quite the star, after your comedy turn." He reined aside, grinning. "What price sympathy on a pagoda?"

For that moment, Rudolph could have struck down the one sure friend he had in China.

CHAPTER VII

IPHIGENIA

"Don't chop off a hen's head with a battle-axe." Heywood, still with a malicious, friendly quirk at the corners of his mouth, held in his fretful pony. Rudolph stood bending a whip viciously. They two had fetched a compass about the town, and now in the twilight were parting before the nunnery gate. "A tiff's the last thing I'd want with you. The lady, in confidence, is not worth--"

"I do not wish," declared Rudolph, trembling,--"I do not wish you to say those things, so!"

"Right!" laughed the other, and his pony wheeled at the word. "I'll give you one month--no: you're such a good, thorough little chap, it will take longer--two months, to change your mind. Only"--he looked down at Rudolph with a comic, elderly air--"let me observe, our yellow people have that rather neat proverb. A hen's head, dear chap,--not with a battle-axe! No. Hot weather's coming, too. No sorrows of Werther, now, over such"--He laughed again. "Don't scowl, I'll be good. I won't say it. You'll supply the word, in two months!"

He let the pony have his way, and was off in a clatter. Lonely, fuming with resentment, Rudolph stared after him. What could he know, this airy, unfeeling meddler, so free with his advice and innuendo? Let him go, then, let him canter away. He had seen quickly, guessed with a diabolic shrewdness, yet would remain on the surface, always, of a mystery so violent and so profound. The young man stalked into his vacant nunnery in a rage, a dismal pomp of emotion: reason telling him that a friend had spoken sense, imagination clothing him in the sceptred pall of tragedy.

Yet one of these unwelcome words had stuck: he was Werther, it was true--a man who came too late. Another word was soon fulfilled; for the hot weather came, sudden, tropical, ferocious. Without gradation, the vernal days and languid noons were gone in a twinkling. The change came like another act of a play. One morning--though the dawn stirred cool and fragrant as all dawns before--the "boy" laid out Rudolph's white tunic, slipped in the shining buttons, smeared pipe-clay on his heaviest helmet; and Rudolph, looking from his window, saw that on the river, by the same instinct, boatmen were stretching up their bamboo awnings. Breakfast was hardly ended, before river, and convex field, and huddling red tiles of the town, lay under a blurred, quivering distortion. The day flamed. At night, against a glow of fiery umber, the western hills broke sharp and thin as sheet-iron, while below them rose in flooding mirage a bright strip of magical water.

Thus, in these days, he rode for his exercise while the sun still lay behind the ocean; and thus her lively, pointed face and wide blue eyes, wondering or downcast or merry, were mingled in his thoughts with the first rousing of the world, the beat of hoofs in cool silences, the wide lights of creation over an aged, weary, alien empire. Their ponies whinnying like old friends, they met, by chance or appointment, before the power of sleep had lifted from eyes still new and strange against the morning. Sometimes Chantel the handsome rode glowering beside them, sometimes Gilly, erect and solid in the saddle, laid upon their talk all the weight of his honest, tired commonplaces.

But one morning she cantered up alone, laughing at her escape. His pony bolted, and they raced along together as comrades happily join forces in a headlong dream. Quivering bamboo swept behind them; the river, on their other hand, met and passed in hurrying panorama. They had no time for words, but only laughter. Words, indeed, had never yet advanced them beyond that moment on the pagoda. And now, when their ponies fell into a shambling trot, came the first impulse of speech.

"How lucky!" she cried. "How lucky we came this way! Now I can really test you!"

He turned. Her glowing face was now averted, her gesture was not for him, but for the scene. He studied that, to understand her.

The river, up which they had fled, now rested broad and quiet as a shallow lake, burnished faintly, brooded over by a floating, increasing light, not yet compounded into day.

Tussocks, innumerable clods and crumbs of vivid green, speckled all the nearer water. On some of these storks meditated,--sage, pondering heads and urbane bodies perched high on the frailest penciling of legs. In the whole expanse, no movement came but when a distant bird, leaving his philosophic pose, plunged downward after a fish. Beyond them rose a shapeless mound or isle, like some half-organic monster grounded in his native ooze.

"There!" said the woman, pointing. "Are you all excuses, like the others? Or do you dare?"

"I am not afraid of anything--now," retorted Rudolph, and with truth, after the dash of their twilight encounter. "Dare what?"

"Go see what's on that island," she answered. "I dared them all. Twice I've seen natives land there and hurry away. Mr. Nesbit was too lazy to try; Dr. Chantel wearing his best clothes. Maurice Heywood refused to mire his horse for a whim. Whim? It's a mystery! Come, now. Do you dare?"

In a rare flush of pride, Rudolph wheeled his stubborn mount and bullied him down the bank. A poor horseman, he would have outstripped Curtius to the gulf. But no sooner had his dancing pony consented to make the first rebellious, sidelong plunge, than he had small joy of his boast. Fore-legs sank floundering, were hoisted with a terrified wrench of the shoulders, in the same moment that hind-legs went down as by suction. The pony squirmed, heaved, wrestled in a frenzy, and churning the red water about his master's thighs, went deeper and fared worse. With a clangor of wings, the storks rose, a streaming rout against the sky, trailed their tilted legs, filed away in straggling flight, like figures interlacing on a panel. At the height of his distress, Rudolph caught a whirling glimpse of the woman above him, safe on firm earth, easy in her saddle, and laughing. Quicksand, then, was a joke,--but he could not pause for this added bewilderment.

The pony, using a skill born of agony, had found somewhere a solid verge and scrambled up, knee-deep, well out from the bank. With a splash, Rudolph stood beside him among the tufts of salad green. As he patted the trembling flanks, he heard a cry from the shore.

"Oh, well done!" she mocked them. "Well done!"

A gust of wholesome anger refreshed him. She might laugh, but now he would see this folly through. He tore off his coat, flung it across the saddle, waded out alone through the tussocks, and shooting forward full length in the turbid water, swam resolutely for the island.

Sky and water brightened while he swam; and as he rose, wrapped in the leaden weight of dripping clothes, the sun, before and above him, touched wonderfully the quaggy bank and parched grasses. He lurched ashore, his feet caked with enormous clods as of melting chocolate. A filthy scramble left him smeared and disheveled on the summit. He had come for nothing. The mound lay vacant, a tangled patch, a fragment of wilderness.

Yet as he stood panting, there rose a puny, miserable sound. What presence could lurk there? The distress, it might be, of some small animal--a rabbit dying in a forgotten trap. Faint as illusion, a wail, a thin-spun thread of sorrow, broke into lonely whimpering, and ceased. He moved forward, doubtfully, and of a sudden, in the scrubby level of the isle, stumbled on the rim of a shallow circular depression.

At first, he could not believe the discovery; but next instant--as at the temple pond, though now without need of placard or interpreter--he understood. This bowl, a tiny crater among the weeds, showed like some paltry valley of Ezekiel, a charnel place of Herod's innocents, the battlefield of some babes' crusade. A chill struck him, not from the water or the early mists. In stupor, he viewed that savage fact.

Through the stillness of death sounded again the note of living discontent. He was aware also of some stir, even before he spied, under a withered clump, the saffron body of an infant girl, feebly squirming. By a loathsome irony, there lay beside her an earthen bowl of rice, as an earnest or symbol of regret.

Blind pity urged him into the atrocious hollow. Seeing no further than the present rescue, he caught up the small unclean sufferer, who moaned the louder as he carried her down the bank, and waded out through the sludge. To hold the squalling mouth above water, and swim, was no simple feat; yet at last he came floundering among the tussocks, wrapped the naked body in his jacket, and with infinite pains tugged his terrified pony along a tortuous bar to the land.

Once in the river-path, he stood gloomily, and let Mrs. Forrester canter up to join him. Indeed, he had almost forgotten her.

"Splendid!" she laughed. "What a figure of fun! But what can you have brought back? Oh, please! I can't wait!"

He turned on her a muddy, haggard face, without enthusiasm, and gently unfolded the coat. The man and the woman looked down together, in silence, at the child. He had some foolish hope that she would take it, that his part was ended. Like an outlandish doll, with face contorted and thick-lidded eyes shut tightly against the sunshine, the outcast whimpered, too near the point of death for even the rebellion of arms and legs.

The woman in the saddle gave a short, incredulous cry. Her face, all gay curiosity, had darkened in a shock of disgust.

"What in the world!" she scolded. "Oh! Such a nasty little-- Why did--What do you propose doing with it?"

Rudolph shook his head, like a man caught in some stupid blunder.

"I never thought of that," he explained heavily. "She has no--no friends."

"Cover it," his companion ordered. "Cover it up. I can't bear to see it."

With a sombre, disappointed air, he obeyed; then looked up, as if in her face he read strange matter.

"I can't bear," she added quickly, "to see any kind of suffering. Why did--It's all my fault for sending you! We were having such a good ride together, and now I've spoiled it all, with this.--Poor little filthy object!" She turned her hands outward, with a helpless, dainty gesture. "But what can we do? These things happen every day."

Rudolph was studying the ground again. His thoughts, then, had wronged her. Drenched and downhearted, holding this strange burden in his jacket, he felt that he had foolishly meddled in things inevitable, beyond repair. She was right.

Yet some vague, insurgent instinct, which would not down, told him that there had been a disappointment. Still, what had he expected? No woman could help; no woman.

Then suddenly he mounted, bundle and all, and turned his willing pony homeward.

"Come," he said; and for the first time, unwittingly, had taken charge.

"What is it?" she called. "You foolish boy! What's your plan?"

"We shall see," he answered. Without waiting, he beckoned her to follow. She came. They rode stirrup to stirrup, silent as in their escape at dawn, and as close bodily, but in spirit traveling distant parallels. He gave no thought to that, riding toward his experiment. Near the town, at last, he reined aside to a cluster of buildings,--white walls and rosy tiles under a great willow.

"You may save your steps," she declared, with sudden petulance. "The hospital's more out of funds than ever, and more crowded. They'll not thank you."

Rudolph nodded back at her, with a queer smile, half reckless and half confident.

"Then," he replied, dismounting, "I will replenish my nunnery."

Squatting coolies sprang up and raced to hold his pony. Others, in the shade of the wall, cackled when they saw a Son of the Red-Haired so beplastered and sopping. A few pointed at his bundle, with grunts of sudden interest; and a leper, bearing the visage as of a stone lion defaced by time, cried something harshly. At his words, the whole band of idlers began to chatter.

Rudolph turned to aid his companion. She sat watching them sharply. An uneasy light troubled the innocent blue eyes, which had not even a glance for him.

"No, I shan't get down," she said angrily. "It's just what might be--Your little brat will bring no good to any of us."

He flung away defiantly, strode through the gate, and calling aloud, traversed an empty compound, already heated by the new-risen sun. A cooler fringe of veranda, or shallow cloister, lined a second court. Two figures met him,--the dark-eyed Miss Drake, all in white, and behind her a shuffling, grinning native woman, who carried a basin, in which permanganate of potash swam gleaming like diluted blood.

"Good-morning." With one droll look of amusement, the girl had understood, and regained that grave yet happy, friendly composure which had the virtue, he discovered, of being easily forgotten, to be met each time like something new. "What have you there for us?"

Again he unfolded the jacket.

"A child."

The naked mite lay very still, the breath weakly fluttered. A somewhat nauseous gift, the girl raised her arms and received it gently, without haste,--the saffron body appearing yet more squalid against the Palladian whiteness of her tunic, plain and cool as drapery in marble.

"It may live," she said. "We'll do what we can." And followed by the black-trousered woman, she moved quickly away to offer battle with death. A plain, usual fact, it seemed, involving no more surprise than repugnance. Her face had hardly altered; and yet Rudolph, for the first time in many days, had caught the fleeting brightness of compassion. Mere light of the eyes, a half-imagined glory, incongruous in the sharp smell of antiseptics, it left him wondering in the cloister. He knew now what had been missing by the river. "I was naked, and"--how ran the lines? He turned to go, recalling in a whirl snatches of truth he had never known since boyhood, never seen away from home.

Across a court the padre hailed him,--a tall, ungainly patriarch under an enormous mushroom helmet of solar pith,--and walking along beside, listened shrewdly to his narrative. They paused at the outer gate. The padre, nodding, frowning slightly, stood at ease, all angles and loose joints, as if relaxed by the growing heat.

Suddenly he stood erect as a grenadier.

"That lie again!" he cried. "Listen!"

The leper, without, harangued from his place apart, in a raucous voice filled with the solitary pride of intellect.

"Well, men shall revile you," growled Dr. Earle. "He says we steal children, to puncture their eyes for magic medicine!"

Then, heaving his wide shoulders,--

"Oh, well!" he said wearily, "thanks, anyhow. Come see us, when we're not so busy? Good!--Look out these fellows don't fly at you."

Tired and befouled, Rudolph passed through into the torrid glare. The leper cut short his snarling oration. But without looking at him, the young man took the bridle from the coolie. There had been a test. He had seen a child, and two women. And yet it was with a pang he found that Mrs. Forrester had not waited.

CHAPTER VIII

THE HOT NIGHT

Rudolph paced his long chamber like a wolf,--a wolf in summer, with too thick a coat. In sweat of body and heat of mind, he crossed from window to window, unable to halt.

A faintly sour smell of parched things, oppressing the night without breath or motion, was like an interminable presence, irritating, poisonous. The punkah, too, flapped incessant, and only made the lamp gutter. Broad leaves outside shone in mockery of snow; and like snow the stifled river lay in the moonlight, where the wet muzzles of buffaloes glistened, floating like knots on sunken logs, or the snouts of crocodiles. Birds fluttered, sleepless and wretched. Coolies, flung asleep on the burnt grass, might have been corpses, but for the sound of their troubled breathing.

"If I could believe," he groaned, sitting with hands thrust through his hair. "If I believe in her--But I came too late,"

The lamp was an added torment. He sprang up from it, wiped the drops off his forehead, and paced again. He came too late. All alone. The collar of his tunic strangled him. He stuffed his fingers underneath, and wrenched; then as he came and went, catching sight in a mirror, was shocked to see that, in Biblical fashion, he had rent his garments.

"This is bad," he thought, staring. "It is the heat. I must not stay alone."

He shouted, clapped his hands for a servant, and at last, snatching a coat from his unruffled boy, hurried away through stillness and moonlight to the detested club. On the stairs a song greeted him,--a fragment with more breath than melody, in a raw bass:--

"Jolly boating weather,
And a hay harvest breeze!"

"Shut up!" snarled another voice. "Good God, man!"

The loft was like a cave heated by subterranean fires. Two

long punkahs flapped languidly in the darkness, with a whine of pulleys. Under a swinging lamp, in a pool of light and heat, four men sat playing cards, their tousled heads, bare arms, and cinglets torn open across the chest, giving them the air of desperadoes.

"Jolly boating weather," wheezed the fat Sturgeon. He stood apart in shadow, swaying on his feet. "What would you give," he propounded thickly, "for a hay harvest breeze?"

He climbed, or rolled, upon the billiard-table, turned head toward punkah, and suddenly lay still,--a gross white figure, collapsed and sprawling.

"How much does he think a man can stand?" snapped Nesbit, his lean Cockney face pulled in savage lines. "Beast of a song! He'll die to-night, drinking."

"Die yourself," mumbled the singer, "'m goin' sleep. More 'n you can do."

A groan from the players, and the vicious flip of a card, acknowledged the hit. Rudolph joined them, ungreeting and ungreeted. The game went on grimly, with now and then the tinkle of ice, or the popping of soda bottles. Sharp cords and flaccid folds in Wutzler's neck, Chantel's brown cheeks, the point of Heywood's resolute chin, shone wet and polished in the lamplight. All four men scowled pugnaciously, even the pale Nesbit, who was winning. Bad temper filled the air, as palpable as the heat and stink of the burning oil.

Only Heywood maintained a febrile gayety, interrupting the game perversely, stirring old Wutzler to incoherent speech.

"What's that about Rome?" he asked. "You were saying?"

"Rome is safed!" cried the outcast, with sudden enthusiasm. "In your paper *Tit-bit*, I read. How dey climb der walls op, yes, but Rome is safed by a flook of geeze. Gracious me, der History iss great sopjeck! I lern moch.--But iss Rome yet a fortify town?"

Chantel rapped out a Parisian oath.

"Do we play cards," he cried sourly, "or listen to the chatter of senility?"

Heywood held to the previous question.

"No, Wutz, that town's no longer fortified," he answered slowly. "Geese live there, still, as in--many other places."

Dr. Chantel examined his finger-tips as though for some defect; then, snatching up the cards, shuffled and dealt with intense precision. The game went on as before.

"I read alzo," stammered Wutzler, like a timid scholar encouraged to lecture, "I read zo how your Englishman, Rawf Ralli, he spreadt der fine clock for your Queen, and lern your Queen smoking, no?" He mopped his lean throat with the back of his hand. "In Bengal are dere Rallis. Dey handle jute."

"Yes?" Heywood smiled a weary indulgence. Next instant he whirled on Rudolph in fury.--"Is this a game, or Idiot's Joy?"

"I'm playing my best," explained Rudolph, sulkily.

"Then your best is the worst I ever saw! Better learn, before sitting in!"

Chantel laughed, without merriment; Rudolph flung down his cards, stalked to the window, and stood looking out, in lonely, impotent rage. A long time passed, marked by alarming snores from the billiard-table. The half-naked watchers played on, in ferocious silence. The night wore along without relief.

Hours might have lapsed, when Dr. Chantel broke out as though the talk had but paused a moment.

"So it goes!" he sneered. "Fools will always sit in, when they do not know. They rush into the water, also, and play the hero!"

Again his laughter was brief but malignant. Heywood had left his cards, risen, and crossing the room, stood looking over Rudolph's shoulder into the snowy moonlight. On the shoulder his hand rested, as by accident.

"It's the heat, old chap," he said wearily. "Don't mind what we say to-night."

Rudolph made no sign, except to move from under his hand, so that, with their quarrel between them, the two men stared out across the blanched roofs and drooping trees, where long black shadows at last crept toward the dawn.

"These heroes!" continued the mocker. "What is danger? Pouf--nothing! They make it for the rest of us, so easily! Do you know," his voice rose and quickened, "do you know, the other end of town is in an uproar? We murder children, it appears, for medicine!"

Rudolph started, turned, but now sat quiet under Heywood's grasp. Chantel, in the lamplight, watched the punkahs with a hateful smile.

"The Gascons are not all dead," he murmured. "They plunge us all into a turmoil, for the sake of a woman." He made a sudden startling gesture, like a man who has lost control. "For the sake," he cried angrily, "of a person we all know! Oh! we all know her! She is nothing more--",

There was a light scuffle at the window.

"Dr. Chantel," began Heywood, with a sharp and dangerous courtesy, "we are all unlike ourselves to-night. I am hardly the person to remind you, but this club is hardly the place--"

"Oh, la la!" The other snapped his fingers, and reverting to his native tongue, finished his sentence wildly.

"You cad!" Heywood advanced in long strides deliberately, as if gathering momentum for a collision. Before his blow could fall, he was sent spinning. Rudolph, his cheeks on fire, darted past and dealt, full force, a clumsy backhand sweep of the arm. Light and quick as a leopard, Chantel was on foot, erect, and even while his chair crashed on the floor, had whipped out a handkerchief.

"You are right, Mr. Heywood," he said, stanching his lips, in icy composure. His eyes held an odd gleam of satisfaction. "You are right. We are not like ourselves, at present. I will better ask Mr. Sturgeon to see your friend to-morrow morning. This morning, rather."

Not without dignity, he turned, stepped quickly to the stairs, saluted gravely, and went down.

"No, no!" panted Nesbit, wrestling with Rudolph. "Easy on, now! Let you go? No fear!"

Heywood wrenched the captive loose, but only to shake him

violently, and thrust him into a chair.

"Be quiet, you little ass!" he scolded. "I've a great mind, myself, to run after the bounder and kick him. But that sort of thing--you did enough. Who'd have thought? You young spitfire! Chantel took you on, exactly as he wanted."

The fat sleeper continued to snore. Wutzler came slinking back from his refuge in the shadows.

"It iss zo badt!" he whined, gulping nervously. "It iss zo badt!"

"Right you are," said Heywood. With arms folded, he eyed them sternly. "It's bad. We might have known. If only I'd reached him first! By Jove, you must let me fight that beast. Duels? The idiot, nobody fights duels any more. I've always--His cuffs are always dirty, too, on the inside!"

Rudolph leaned back, like a man refreshed and comforted, but his laugh was unsteady, and too boisterous.

"It is well," he bragged. "Pistol-bullets--they fly on the wings of chance! No?--All is well."

"Pistols? My dear young gentleman," scoffed his friend, "there's not a pair of matched pistols in the settlement. And if there were, Chantel has the choice. He'll take swords."

He paused, in a silence that grew somewhat menacing. From a slit in the wall the wheel of the punkah-thong whined insistently,--rise and fall, rise and fall of peevish complaint, distressing as a brain-fever bird.

"Swords, of course," continued Heywood. "If only out of vanity. Fencing,--oh, I hate the man, and the art's by-gone, if you like, but he's a beautiful swordsman! Wonderful!"

Rudolph still lay back, but now with a singular calm.

"It's just as well," he declared quietly.

Heywood loosed a great breath, a sigh of vast relief.

"My word!" he cried, grinning. "So you're there, too, eh? You young Sly-boots! If you're another expert--Bravo! We'll beat him at his own game! Hoist with his own what-d'-ye-call-it! I'd give anything"--He thumped the table, and pitched the cards broadcast, like an explosion of confetti, in a little carnival of glee. "You old Sly-boots!--But are you sure? He's quick as lightning."

"I am not afraid," replied Rudolph, modestly. He trained his young moustache upward with steady fingers, and sat very quiet, thinking long thoughts. A quaint smile played about his eyes.

"Good for you!" said Heywood. "Now let him come, as the Lord Mayor said of the hare. What sport! With an even chance--And what a load off one's mind!"

He moved away to the window, as though searching for air. Instead of moonlight, without, there swam the blue mist of dawn.

"Not a word must ever reach old Gilly," he mused. "Do you hear, Nesbit?"

"If you think," retorted the clerk, stiffly, "I don't know the proper course of be'aviour! Not likely!"

The tall silhouette in the window made no reply, but stood grumbling privately: "A club! Yes, where we drink out of jam-pots--dead cushions, dead balls--no veranda--fellow that soils the inside of his cuffs first! We're a pack of beach-combers."

He propped his elbows on the long sill, and leaned out, venting fragments of disgust. Then of a sudden he turned, and beckoned eagerly. "Come here, you chaps. Look-see."

The others joined him. Gray vapors from river and paddy-field, lingering like steam in a slow breeze, paled and dispersed in the growing light, as the new day, worse than the old, came sullenly without breath or respite. A few twilight shapes were pattering through the narrow street--a squad of Yamên runners haling a prisoner.

"The Sword-Pen remains active," said Heywood, thoughtfully. "That dingy little procession, do you know, it's quite theatrical? The Cross and the Dragon. Eh? Another act's coming."

Even Rudolph could spare a misgiving from his own difficulty while he watched the prisoner. It was Chok Chung, the plump Christian merchant, slowly trudging toward the darkest of human courts, to answer for the death of the cormorant-fisher. The squad passed by. Rudolph saw again the lighted shop, the tumbled figure retching on the floor; and with these came a memory of that cold and scornful face, thinking so cruelly among the unthinking rabble. The Sword-Pen had written something in the dark.

"I go find out"; and Wutzler was away, as keen as a village gossip.

"Trouble's comin'," Nesbit asserted glibly. "There's politics afloat. But I don't care." He stretched his arms, with a weary howl. "That's the first yawn I've done to-night. Trouble keeps, worse luck. I'm off--seek my downy."

Alone with the grunting sleeper, the two friends sat for a long time and watched the flooding daylight.

"What," began Rudolph, suddenly, and his voice trembled, "what is your true opinion? You are so kind, and I was just a fool. That other day, I would not listen. You laughed. Now tell me, so--as you were to die next. You were joking? Can I truly be proud of--of her?"

He leaned forward, white and eager, waiting for the truth like a dicer for the final throw.

"Of yourself, dear old chap. Not of the lady. She's the fool, not you. Poor old Gilly Forrester slaves here to send her junketing in Japan, Kashmir, Ceylon, Home. What Chantel said--well, between the two of us, I'm afraid he's right. It's a pity."

Heywood paused, frowning.

"A pity, too, this quarrel. So precious few of us, and trouble ahead. The natives lashing themselves into a state of mind, or being lashed. The least spark--Rough work ahead, and here we are at swords' points."

"And the joke is," Rudolph added quietly, "I do not know a sword's point from a handle."

Heywood turned, glowered, and twice failed to speak.

"Rudie--old boy," he stammered, "that man--Preposterous! Why, it's plain murder!"

Rudolph stared straight ahead, without hope, without illusions, facing the haggard light of morning. A few weeks ago he might have wept; but now his laugh, short and humorous, was worthy of his companion.

"I do not care, more," he answered. "Luck, so called I it, when I escaped the militar' service. Ho ho! Luck, to pass into the *Ersatz!*--I do not care, now. I cannot believe, even cannot I fight. Worthless--dreamer! My deserts. It's a good way out."

CHAPTER IX

PASSAGE AT ARMS

"Boy."

"Sai."

"S'pose Mr. Forrester bym-by come, you talkee he, master no got, you chin-chin he come-back."

"Can do."

The long-coated boy scuffed away, across the chunam floor, and disappeared in the darkness. Heywood submitted his head once more to the nimble hands of his groom, who, with horse-clippers and a pair of enormous iron shears, was trimming the stubborn chestnut locks still closer. The afternoon glow, reflected from the burnt grass and white walls of the compound, struck upward in the vault-spaces of the ground floor, and lighted oddly the keen-eyed yellow mafoo and his serious young master.

Nesbit, pert as a jockey, sat on the table swinging his feet furiously.

"Sturgeon would take it all right, of course," he said, with airy wisdom. "Quite the gentleman, he is. Netch'rally. No fault of his."

"Not the least," Heywood assented gloomily. "Did everything he could. If I were commissioned to tell 'em outright--'The youngster can't fence'--why, we might save the day. But our man won't even listen to that. Fight's the word. Chantel will see, on the spot, directly they face. But will that stop him? No fear: he's worked up to the pitch of killing. He'll lunge first, and be surprised afterward.--So regrettable! Such remorse!--Oh, I know *him!*"

The Cockney fidgeted for a time. His face--the face of a street-bred urchin--slowly worked into lines of abnormal cunning.

"I say! I was thinking," he ventured at last. "Two swords, that's all? Just so. Now--my boy used to be learn-pidgin at Chantel's. Knows that 'ouse inside out--loafs there now, the

beggar, with Chantel's cook. Why not send him over--
prowling, ye know--fingers the bric-a-brac, bloomin' ass,
and breaks a sword-blade. Perfectly netch'ral. 'Can secure, all
plopah,' Accident, ye know. All off with their little duel.
What?"

Heywood chuckled, and bowed his head to the horse-
clippers.

"Last week," he replied. "Not to-day. This afternoon's rather
late for accidents. You make me feel like Pompey on his
galley: 'This thou shouldst have done, and not have spoken
on't,'--Besides, those swords belonged to Chantel's father.
He began as a gentleman.--But you're a good sort, Nesbit, to
take the affair this fashion."

Lost in smoke, the clerk grumbled that the gory affair was
unmentionable nonsense.

"Quite," said Heywood. "We've tried reasoning. No go. As
you say, an accident. That's all can save the youngster now.
Impossible, of course." He sighed. Then suddenly the gray
eyes lighted, became both shrewd and distant; a malicious
little smile stole about the corners of his mouth. "Have-got!
The credit's yours, Nesbit. Accident: can do. And this one--
by Jove, it won't leave either of 'em a leg to stand on!--Here,
mafoo, makee finish!"

He sprang up, clapped a helmet on the shorn head, and
stalked out into the sunlight.

"Come on," he called. "It's nearly time. We must pick up
our young Hotspur."

The clerk followed, through the glowing compound and the
road. In the shade of the nunnery gate they found Rudolph,
who, raising his rattan, saluted them with a pale and stoic
gravity.

"Are we ready?" he asked; and turning, took a slow, cool
survey of the nunnery, as though looking his last--from the
ditch at their feet to the red tiles, patched with bronze
mould, that capped the walls and the roof. "I never left any
place with less regret. Come, let's go."

The three men had covered some ground before Rudolph
broke the silence.

"You'll find a few little things up there in my strong-box, Maurice. Some are marked for you, and the rest--will you send them Home, please?" He hesitated. "I hope neither of you will misunderstand me. I'm horribly afraid, but not--but only because this fellow will make me look absurd. If I knew the first motion!" He broke out angrily. "I cannot bear to have him laugh, also! I cannot bear!"

Heywood clapped him on the shoulder, and gave a queer cough.

"If that's all, never you fear! I'll teach you your guard. 'Once in a while we can finish in style.' Eh?--Rudie, you blooming German, I--I think we must have been brothers! We'll pull it off yet."

Heywood spoke with a strange alacrity, and tried again to cough. This time, however, there was no mistake--he was laughing.

Rudolph shot at him one glance of startled unbelief, and then, tossing his head, marched on without a word. Pride and loneliness overwhelmed him. The two at his side were no companions--not even presences. He went alone, conscious only of the long flood of sunset, and the black interlacing pattern of bamboos. The one friendly spirit had deserted, laughing; yet even this last and worst of earthly puzzles did not matter. It was true, what he had read; this, which they called death, was a lonely thing.

On a broken stone bench, Sturgeon, sober and dejected, with puffy circles under his eyes, sat waiting. A long parcel, wrapped in green baize, lay across his knees. He nodded gloomily, without rising. At his feet wandered a path, rankly matted with burnt weeds, and bordered with green bottle-ends, the "dimples" choked with discs of mud. The place was a deserted garden, where the ruins of a European house--burnt by natives in some obscure madness, years ago--sprawled in desolation among wild shrubs. A little way down the path stood Teppich and Chantel, each with his back turned and his hands clasped, like a pair of sulky Napoleons, one fat, one slender. The wooden pretense of their attitude set Rudolph, for an instant, to laughing silently and bitterly. This final scene,--what justice, that it should be a mean waste, the wreck of silly pleasure-grounds, long forgotten, and now used only by grotesque play-actors. He must die, in both action and setting, without dignity. It was some comfort, he became aware, to find that the place was fairly private. Except for the breach by which they had entered, the blotched and spotted compound walls stood ruinous yet high, shutting out all but a rising slant of sunlight, and from some outpost line of shops, near by, the rattle of an abacus and the broken singsong of argument, now harsh, now drowsy.

Heywood had been speaking earnestly to Sturgeon:--

"A little practice--try the balance of the swords. No more than fair."

"Fair? Most certainly," croaked that battered convivialist. "Chantel can't object."

He rose, and waddled down the path. Rudolph saw Chantel turn, frowning, then nod and smile. The nod was courteous, the smile full of satire. The fat ambassador returned.

"Right-oh," he puffed, tugging from the baize cover a shining pair of bell-hilted swords. "Here, try 'em out." His puffy eyes turned furtively toward Rudolph. "May be bad form, Hackh, but--we all wish you luck, I fancy." Then, in a burst of candor, "Wish that unspeakable ass felt as seedy as I do--heat-stroke--drop dead--that sort of thing."

Still grumbling treason, this strange second rejoined his principal.

"Jackets off," commanded Heywood; and in their cinglets, each with sword under arm, the two friends took shelter behind a ragged clump of plantains. The yellow leaves, half dead with drought and blight, hung ponderous as torn strips of sheet metal in the lifeless air.

Behind this tattered screen, Rudolph studied, for a moment, the lethal object in his hand. It was very graceful,--the tapering, three-cornered blade, with shallow grooves in which blood was soon to run, the silver hilt where his enemy's father had set, in florid letters, the name of "H.B. St. A. Chantel," and a date. How long ago, he thought, the steel was forged for this day.

"It is Fate." He looked up sadly. "Come, show me how to

begin; so that I can stand up to him."

"Here, then." Slowly, easily, his long limbs transformed with a sudden youthful grace, Heywood moved through the seven positions of On Guard. "Try it."

Rudolph learned only that his own clumsy imitation was hopeless.

"Once more.--He can't see us."

Again and again, more and more rapidly, they performed the motions of this odd rehearsal. Suddenly Heywood stepped back, and lowering his point, looked into his pupil's face, long and earnestly.

"For the last time," he said: "won't you let me tell him? This is extremely silly."

Rudolph hung his head, like a stubborn child.

"Do you still think," he answered coldly, "that I would beg off?"

With a hopeless gesture of impatience, Heywood stepped forward briskly. "Very well, then. Once more." And as their blades clashed softly together, a quick light danced in his eyes. "Here's how our friend will stick you!" His point cut a swift little circle, and sped home. By a wild instinct, the novice beat it awkwardly aside. His friend laughed, poised again, disengaged again, but in mid-career of this heartless play, stumbled and came pitching forward. Rudolph darted back, swept his arm blindly, and cried out; for with the full impetus of the mishap, a shock had run from wrist to elbow. He dropped his sword, and in stupefaction watched the red blood coursing down his forearm, and his third finger twitching convulsively, beyond control.

"Dear fellow!" cried his opponent, scrambling upright. "So sorry! I say, that's a bad one." With a stick and a handkerchief, he twisted on a tourniquet, muttering condolence: "Pain much? Lost my balance, you know. That better?--What a clumsy accident!" Then, dodging out from the plantain screen, and beckoning,--"All you chaps! Come over here!"

Nesbit came running, but at sight of the bloody victim, pulled up short. "What ho!" he whispered, first with a stare, then a grin of mysterious joy. Sturgeon gave a sympathetic whistle, and stolidly unwound bandages. At first the two Napoleons remained aloof, but at last, yielding to indignant shouts, haughtily approached. The little group stood at fault.

Heywood wiped his sword-blade very carefully on a plantain leaf; then stood erect, to address them with a kind of cool severity.

"I regret this more than anybody," he declared, pausing, and picking his words. "We were at practice, and my friend had the misfortune to be run through the arm."

Chantel flung out his hands, in a motion at once furious and impudent.

"Zut! What a farce!--Will you tell me, please, since your friend has disabled himself"--

Heywood wheeled upon him, scornfully.

"You have no right to such an expression," he stated, with a coldness which conveyed more rage than the other man's heat. "This was entirely my fault. It's I who have spoiled your--arrangement, and therefore I am quite ready to take up my friend's quarrel."

"I have no quarrel with you," replied Chantel, contemptuously. "You saw last night how he--"

"He was quicker than I, that's all. By every circumstance, I'm the natural proxy. Besides"--the young man appealed to the company, smiling--"besides, what a pity to postpone matters, and spoil the occasion, when Doctor Chantel has gone to the trouble of a clean shirt."

The doctor recoiled, flung up a trembling arm, and as quickly dropped it. His handsome face burned darker, then faded with a mortal pallor, and for one rigid moment, took on such a strange beauty as though it were about to be translated into bronze. His brown fingers twitched, became all nerves and sinews and white knuckles. Then, stepping backward, he withdrew from the circle.

"Very well," he said lightly. "Since we are all so--irregular. I will take the substitute."

Rudolph gave a choking cry, and would have come forward;

but Sturgeon clung to the wounded arm, and bound on his bandage.

"Hold still, there!" he scolded, as though addressing a horse; then growled inHeywood's ear, "Why did *you* go lose your temper?"

"Didn't. We can't let him walk over us, though." The young man held the sword across his throat, and whispered, "Only angry up to here!"

And indeed, through the anxious preliminary silence, he stood waiting as cool and ready as a young centurion.

His adversary, turning back the sleeves of the unfortunate white linen, picked up the other sword, and practiced his fingering on the silver hilt, while the blade answered as delicately as the bow to a violinist. At last he came forward, with thin lips and hard, thoughtful eyes, like a man bent upon dispatch. Both men saluted formally, and sprang on guard.

From the first twitter of the blades, even Rudolph knew the outcome. Heywood, his face white and anxious in the failing light, fought at full stretch, at the last wrench of skill. Chantel, for the moment, was fencing; and though his attacks came ceaseless and quick as flame, he was plainly prolonging them, discarding them, repeating, varying, whether for black-hearted merriment, or the vanity of perfect form, or love of his art. Graceful, safe, easy, as though performing the grand salute, he teased and frolicked, his bright blade puzzling the sight, scattering like quicksilver in the endless whirl and clash.

Teppich was gaping foolishly, Sturgeon shaking his head, the Cockney, with narrow body drawn together, watching, shivering, squatting on toes and finger-tips, like a runner about to spring from a mark. Rudolph, dizzy with pain and suspense, nursed his forearm mechanically. The hurried, silver ring of the hilts dismayed him, the dust from the garden path choked him like an acrid smoke.

Suddenly Chantel, dropping low like a deflected arrow, swooped in with fingers touching the ground. On "three feet," he had delivered the blow so long withheld.

The watchers shouted. Nesbit sprang up, released. But

Heywood, by some desperate sleight, had parried the
certainty, and even tried a riposte. Still afoot and fighting, he
complained testily above the sword-play:--

"Don't shout like that! Fair field, you chaps!"

Above the sword-play, too, came gradually a murmur of
voices. Through the dust, beyond the lunging figures,
Rudolph was distantly aware of crowded bodies, of yellow
faces grinning or agape, in the breach of the compound wall.
Men of the neighboring hamlet had gathered, to watch the
foreign monsters play at this new, fantastic game. Shaven
heads bobbed, saffron arms pointed, voices, sharp and
guttural, argued scornfully.

The hilts rang, the blades grated faster. But now it was plain
that Heywood could do no more, by luck or inspiration.
Fretted by his clumsy yet strong and close defense, Chantel
was forcing on the end. He gave a panting laugh. Instantly,
all saw the weaker blade fly wide, the stronger swerve, to
dart in victorious,--and then saw Doctor Chantel staggering
backward, struck full in the face by something round and
heavy. The brown missile skipped along the garden path.

RUDOLPH WAS AWARE OF CROWDED BODIES, OF
YELLOW FACES GRINNING

Another struck a bottle-end, and burst into milk-white fragments, like a bomb. A third, rebounding from Teppich's girdle, left him bent and gasping. Strange yells broke out, as from a tribe of apes. The air was thick with hurtling globes. Cocoanuts rained upon the company, tempestuously, as though an invisible palm were shaken by a hurricane. Among them flew sticks, jagged lumps of sun-dried clay, thick scales of plaster.

"Aow!" cried Nesbit, "the bloomin' coolies!" First to recover, he skipped about, fielding and hurling back cocoanuts.

A small but raging phalanx crowded the gap in the wall, throwing continually, howling, and exhorting one another to rush in.

"A riot!" cried Heywood, and started, sword in hand. "Come on, stop 'em!"

But it was Nesbit who, wrenching a pair of loose bottles from the path, brandishing them aloft like clubs, and shouting the unseemly battle-cries of a street-fighter, led the white men into this deadly breach. At the first shock, the rioters broke and scattered, fled round corners of the wall, crashed through bamboos, went leaping across paddy-fields toward the river. The tumult--except for lonely howls in the distance--ended as quickly as it had risen. The little band of Europeans returned from the pursuit, drenched with sweat, panting, like a squad of triumphant football players; but no one smiled.

"That explains it," grumbled Heywood. He pointed along the path to where, far off, a tall, stooping figure paced slowly toward the town, his long robe a moving strip of color, faint in the twilight. "The Sword-Pen dropped some remarks in passing."

The others nodded moodily, too breathless for reply. Nesbit's forehead bore an ugly cut, Rudolph's bandage was red and sopping. Chantel, more rueful than either, stared down at a bleeding hand, which held two shards of steel. He had fallen, and snapped his sword in the rubble of old masonry.

"No more blades," he said, like a child with a broken toy; "there are no more blades this side of Saigon."

"Then we must postpone." Heywood mopped his dripping and fiery cheeks. He tossed a piece of silver to one who wailed in the ditch,--a forlorn stranger from Hai-nan, lamenting the broken shells and empty baskets of his small venture.--"Contribution, you chaps. A bad day for imported cocoanuts. Wish I carried some money: this chit system is damnable.--Meanwhile, doctor, won't you forget anything I was rude enough to say? And come join me in a peg at the club? The heat is excessive."

CHAPTER X

THREE PORTALS

Not till after dinner, that evening, did Rudolph rouse from his stupor. With the clerk, he lay wearily in the upper chamber of Heywood's house. The host, with both his long legs out at window, sat watching the smoky lights along the river, and now and then cursing the heat.

"After all," he broke silence, "those cocoanuts came time enough."

"Didn't they just?" said Nesbit, jauntily; and fingering the plaster cross on his wounded forehead, drawled: "You might think I'd done a bit o' dueling myself, by the looks.--But I had *some* part. Now, that accident trick. Rather neat, what? But for me, you might never have thought o' that--"

"Idiot!" snapped Heywood, and pulling in his legs, rose and stamped across the room.

A glass of ice and tansan smashed on the floor. Rudolph was on foot, clutching his bandaged arm as though the hurt were new.

"You!" he stammered. "You did that!" He stood gaping, thunderstruck.

Felt soles scuffed in the darkness, and through the door, his yellow face wearing a placid and lofty grin, entered Ah Pat, the compradore.

"One coolie-man hab-got chit."

He handed a note to his master, who snatched it as though glad of the interruption, bent under the lamp, and scowled.

The writing was in a crabbed, antique German character:--

"Please to see bearer, in bad clothes but urgent. We are all in danger. *Um Gottes willen--*" It straggled off, illegible. The signature, "Otto Wutzler," ran frantically into a blot.

"Can do," said Heywood. "You talkee he, come topside."

The messenger must have been waiting, however, at the

stairhead; for no sooner had the compradore withdrawn, than a singular little coolie shuffled into the room. Lean and shriveled as an opium-smoker, he wore loose clothes of dirty blue,--one trousers-leg rolled up. The brown face, thin and comically small, wore a mask of inky shadow under a wicker bowl hat. His eyes were cast down in a strange fashion, unlike the bold, inquisitive peering of his countrymen,--the more strange, in that he spoke harshly and abruptly, like a racer catching breath.

"I bring news." His dialect was the vilest and surliest form of the colloquial "Clear Speech."--"One pair of ears, enough."

"You can speak and act more civilly," retorted Heywood, "or taste the bamboo."

The man did not answer, or look up, or remove his varnished hat. Still downcast and hang-dog, he sidled along the verge of the shadow, snatched from the table the paper and a pencil, and choosing the darkest part of the wall, began to write. The lamp stood between him and the company: Heywood alone saw--and with a shock of amazement--that he did not print vertically as with a brush, but scrawled horizontally. He tossed back the paper, and dodged once more into the gloom.

The postscript ran in the same shaky hand:--

"Send way the others both."

"What!" cried the young master of the house; and then over his shoulder, "Excuse us a moment--me, I should say."

He led the dwarfish coolie across the landing, to the deserted dinner-table. The creature darted past him, blew out one candle, and thrust the other behind a bottle, so that he stood in a wedge of shadow.

"Eng-lish speak I ver' badt," he whispered; and then with something between gasp and chuckle, "but der *pak-wa* goot, no? When der live dependt, zo can mann--" He caught his breath, and trembled in a strong seizure.

"Good?" whisperedHeywood, staring. "Why, man, it's wonderful! You *are* a coolie"--Wutzler's conical wicker-hat ducked as from a blow. "I beg your pardon. I mean, you're--

"

The shrunken figure pulled itself together.

"You are right," he whispered, in the vernacular. "To-night I am a coolie--all but the eyes. Therefore this hat."

Heywood stepped back to the door, and popped his head out. The dim hall was empty.

"Go on," he said, returning. "What is your news?"

"Riots. They are coming. We are all marked for massacre. All day I ran about the town, finding out. The trial of Chok Chung, your--*our* Christian merchant--I saw him 'cross the hall.' They kept asking, 'Do you follow the foreign dogs and goats?' But he would only answer, 'I follow the Lord Jesus.' So then they beat out his teeth with a heavy shoe, and cast him into prison. Now they wait, to see if his padre will interfere with the law. It is a trap. The suit is certainly brought by Fang the scholar, whom they call the Sword-Pen."

"That much," said Heywood, "I could have told you."

Wutzler glanced behind him fearfully, as though the flickering shadows might hear.

"But there is more. Since dark I ran everywhere, watching, listening to gossip. I painted my skin with mangrove-bark water. You know this sign?" He patted his right leg, where the roll of trousers bound his thigh. "It is for protection in the streets. It says, 'I am a Heaven-and-Earth man.'"

"The Triad!" Heywood whistled. "You?"

The other faltered, and hung his head.

"Yes," he whispered at last. "My--my wife's cousin, he is a Grass Sandal. He taught her the verses at home, for safety.-- We mean no harm, now, we of the Triad. But there is another secret band, having many of our signs. It is said they ape our ritual. Fang the scholar heads their lodge. They are the White Lotus."

"White Lotus?" Heywood snapped his fingers. "Nonsense. Extinct, this hundred years."

"Extinct? They meet to-night," said the outcast, in sudden

grief and passion. "They drink blood--plan blood. Extinct? Are *you* married to these people? Does the knowledge come so cheap, or at a price? All these years--darkness--sunken-- alone"--He trembled violently, but regained his voice. "O my friend! This very night they swear in recruits, and set the day. I know their lodge-room. For any sake, believe me! I know!"

"Right," said Heywood, curtly. "I believe you. But why come here? Why not stay, and learn more?"

Wutzler's head dropped on his breast again. The varnished hat gleamed softly in the darkness.

"I--I dare not stay," he sobbed.

"Oh, exactly!" Heywood flung out an impatient arm. "The date, man! The day they set. You came away without it!--We sit tight, then, and wait in ignorance."

The droll, withered face, suddenly raised, shone with great tears that streaked the mangrove stain.

"My head sits loosely already, with what I have done to-night. I found a listening place--next door: a long roof. You can hear and see them--But I could not stay. Yes, I am a coward."

"There, there!" Heywood patted his shoulder. "I didn't mean--Here, have a drink."

The man drained the tumbler at a gulp; stood without a word, sniffing miserably; then of a sudden, as though the draught had worked, looked up bold and shrewd.

"Do you?" he whispered. "Do *you* dare go to the place I show you, and hide? You would learn."

Heywood started visibly, paused, then laughed.

"Excellent," he said. "*Tu quoque* is good argument. Can you smuggle me?--Then come on." He stepped lightly across the landing, and called out, "You chaps make yourselves at home, will you? Business, you know. What a bore! I'll not be back till late." And as he followed the slinking form downstairs, he grumbled, "If at all, perhaps."

The moon still lurked behind the ocean, making an aqueous pallor above the crouching roofs. The two men hurried along a "goat" path, skirted the town wall, and stole through a dark gate into a darker maze of lonely streets. Drawing nearer to a faint clash of cymbals in some joss-house, they halted before a blind wall.

"In the first room," whispered the guide, "a circle is drawn on the floor. Put your right foot there, and say, 'We are all in-the-circle men,' If they ask, remember: you go to pluck the White Lotus. These men hate it, they are Triad brothers, they will let you pass. You come from the East, where the Fusang cocks spit orient pearls; you studied in the Red Flower Pavilion; your eyes are bloodshot because"--He lectured earnestly, repeating desperate nonsense, over and over. "No: not so. Say it exactly, after me."

They held a hurried catechism in the dark.

"There," sighed Wutzler, at last, "that is as much as we can hope. Do not forget. They will pass you through hidden ways.--But you are very rash. It is not too late to go home."

Receiving no answer, he sighed more heavily, and gave a complicated knock. Bars clattered within, and a strip of dim light widened. "Who comes?" said a harsh but guarded voice, with a strong Hakka brogue.

"A brother," answered the outcast, "to pluck the White Lotus. Aid, brothers.--Go in, I can help no further. If you are caught, slide down, and run westward to the gate which is called the Meeting of the Dragons."

Heywood nodded, and slipped in. Beside a leaf-point flame of peanut-oil, a broad, squat giant sat stiff and still against the opposite wall, and stared with cruel, unblinking eyes. If the stranger were the first white man to enter, this motionless grim janitor gave no sign. On the earthen floor lay a small circle of white lime. Heywood placed his right foot inside it.

"We are all in-the-circle men."

"Pass," said the guard.

Out from shadow glided a tall native with a halberd, who opened a door in the far corner.

In the second room, dim as the first, burned the same smoky orange light on the same table. But here a twisted cripple, his nose long and pendulous with elephantiasis, presided over three cups of tea set in a row. Heywood lifted the central cup, and drank.

"Will you bite the clouds?" asked the second guard, in a soft and husky bass. As he spoke, the great nose trembled slightly.

"No, I will bite ginger," replied the white man.

"Why is your face so green?"

"It is a melon-face--a green face with a red heart."

"Pass," said the cripple, gently. He pulled a cord--the nose quaking with this exertion--and opened the third door.

Again the chamber was dim. A venerable man in gleaming silks--a grandfather, by his drooping rat-tail moustaches--sat fanning himself. In the breath of his black fan, the lamplight tossed queer shadows leaping, and danced on the table of polished camagon. Except for this unrest, the aged face might have been carved from yellow soapstone. But his slant eyes were the sharpest yet.

"You have come far," he said, with sinister and warning courtesy.

Too far, thought Heywood, in a sinking heart; but answered:--

"From the East, where the Fusang cocks spit orient pearls."

"And where did you study?" The black fan stopped fluttering.

"In the Red Flower Pavilion."

"What book did you read?"

"The book," said Heywood, holding his wits by his will, "the book was Ten Thousand Thousand Pages."

"And the theme?"

"The waters of the deluge crosswise flow." "And what"--the aged voice rose briskly--"what saw you on the waters?"

"The Eight Abbots, floating," answered Heywood, negligently.--"But," ran his thought, "he'll pump me dry."

"Why," continued the examiner, "do you look so happy?"

"Because Heaven has sent the Unicorn."

The black fan began fluttering once more. It seemed a hopeful sign; but the keen old eyes were far from satisfied.

"Why have you such a sensual face?"

"I was born under a peach tree."

"Pass," said the old man, regretfully. And Heywood, glancing back from the mouth of a dark corridor, saw him, beside the table of camagon, wagging his head like a judge doubtful of his judgment.

The narrow passage, hot, fetid, and blacker than the wholesome night without, crooked about sharp corners, that bruised the wanderer's hands and arms. Suddenly he fell down a short flight of slimy steps, landing in noisome mud at the bottom of some crypt. A trap, a suffocating well, he thought; and rose filthy, choked with bitterness and disgust. Only the taunting justice of Wutzler's argument, the retort *ad hominem*, had sent him headlong into this dangerous folly. He had scolded a coward with hasty words, and been forced to follow where they led. To this loathsome hole. Behind him, a door closed, a bar scraped softly into place. Before him, as he groped in rage and self-reproach, rose a vault of solid plaster, narrow as a chimney.

But presently, glancing upward, he saw a small cluster of stars blinking, voluptuous, immeasurably overhead. Their pittance of light, as his eyesight cleared, showed a ladder rising flat against the wall. He reached up, grasped the bamboo rungs, hoisted with an acrobatic wrench, and began to climb cautiously.

Above, faint and muffled, sounded a murmur of voices.

CHAPTER XI

WHITE LOTUS

He was swarming up, quiet as a thief, when his fingers clawed the bare plaster. The ladder hung from the square end of a protruding beam, above which there were no more rungs. He hung in doubt.

Then, to his great relief, something blacker than the starlight gathered into form over his head,--a slanting bulk, which gradually took on a familiar meaning. He chuckled, reached for it, and fingering the rough edge to avoid loose tiles, hauled himself up to a foothold on the beam, and so, flinging out his arms and hooking one knee, scrambled over and lay on a ribbed and mossy surface, under the friendly stars. The outcast and his strange brethren had played fair: this was the long roof, and close ahead rose the wall of some higher building, an upright blackness from which escaped two bits of light,--a right angle of hairbreadth lines, and below this a brighter patch, small and ragged. Here, louder, but confused with a gentle scuffing of feet, sounded the voices of the rival lodge.

Toward these he crawled, stopping at every creak of the tiles. Once a broken roll snapped off, and slid rattling down the roof. He sat up, every muscle ready for the sudden leap and shove that would send him sliding after it into the lower darkness. It fell but a short distance, into something soft. Gradually he relaxed, but lay very still. Nothing followed; no one had heard.

He tried again, crawled forward his own length, and brought up snug and safe in the angle where roof met wall. The voices and shuffling feet were dangerously close. He sat up, caught a shaft of light full in his face, and peered in through the ragged chink. Two legs in bright, wrinkled hose, and a pair of black shoes with thick white soles, blocked the view. For a long time they shifted, uneasy and tantalizing. He could hear only a hubbub of talk,--random phrases without meaning. The legs moved away, and left a clear space.

But at the same instant, a grating noise startled him, directly overhead, out of doors. The thin right angle of light spread instantly into a brilliant square. With a bang, a wooden shutter slid open. Heywood lay back swiftly, just as a long, fat bamboo pipe, two sleeves, and the head of a man in a red silk cap were thrust out into the night air.

"*Ai-yah!*" sighed the man, and puffed at his bamboo. "It is hot."

Heywood tried to blot himself against the wall. The lounger, propped on elbows, finished his smoke, spat upon the tiles, and remained, a pensive silhouette.

"*Ai-yah!*" he sighed again; then knocking out the bamboo, drew in his head. Not until the shutter slammed, did Heywood shake the burning sparks from his wrist.

In the same movement, however, he raised head and shoulders to spy through the chink. This time the bright-hosed legs were gone. He saw clear down a brilliant lane of robes and banners, multicolored, and shining with embroidery and tinsel,--a lane between two ranks of crowded men, who, splendid with green and blue and yellow robes of ceremony, faced each other in a strong lamplight, that glistened on their oily cheeks. The chatter had ceased. Under the crowded rows of shaven foreheads, their eyes blinked, deep-set and expectant. At the far end of the loft, through two circular arches or giant hoops of rattan, Heywood at last descried a third arch, of swords; beyond this, a tall incense jar smouldering gray wisps of smoke, beside a transverse table twinkling with candles like an altar; and over these, a black image with a pale, carved face, seated bolt upright before a lofty, intricate, gilded shrine of the Patriot War-God.

A tall man in dove-gray silk with a high scarlet turban moved athwart the altar, chanting as he solemnly lifted one by one a row of symbols: a round wooden measure, heaped with something white, like rice, in which stuck a gay cluster of paper flags; a brown, polished abacus; a mace carved with a dragon, another carved with a phoenix; a rainbow robe, gleaming with the plumage of Siamese kingfishers. All these, and more, he displayed aloft and replaced among the candles.

When his chant ended, a brisk little man in yellow stepped

forward into the lane.

"O Fragrant Ones," he shrilled, "I bring ten thousand recruits, to join our army and swear brotherhood. Attend, O Master of Incense."

Behind him, a squad of some dozen barefoot wretches, in coolie clothes, with queues un-plaited, crawled on all fours through the first arch. They crouched abject, while the tall Master of Incense in the dove-gray silk sternly examined their sponsor.

In the outer darkness, Heywood craned and listened till neck and shoulders ached. He could make nothing of the florid verbiage.

With endless ritual, the crawling novices reached the arch of swords. They knelt, each holding above his head a lighted bundle of incense-sticks,--red sparks that quivered like angry fireflies. Above them the tall Master of Incense thundered:--

"O Spirits of the Hills and Brooks, the Land, the swollen seeds of the ground, and all the Veins of Earth; O Thou, young Bearer of the Axe that cleared the Hills; O Imperial Heaven, and ye, Five Dragons of the Five Regions, with all the Holy Influences who pass and instantly re-pass through unutterable space:--draw near, record our oath, accept the draught of blood."

He raised at arm's length a heavy baton, which, with a flowing movement, unrolled to the floor a bright yellow scroll thickly inscribed. From this he read, slowly, an interminable catalogue of oaths. Heywood could catch only the scolding sing-song of the responses:--

"If any brother shall break this, let him die beneath ten thousand knives."

"--Who violates this, shall be hurled down into the great sky."

"--Let thunder from the Five Regions annihilate him."

Silence followed, broken suddenly by the frenzied squawking of a fowl, as suddenly cut short. Near the chink, Heywood heard a quick struggling and beating. Next instant he lay flattened against the wall.

The shutter grated open, a flood of light poured out.

Within reach, in that radiance, a pair of sinewy yellow hands gripped the neck of a white cock. The wretched bird squawked once more, feebly, flapped its wings, and clawed the air, just as a second pair of arms reached out and sliced with a knife. The cock's head flew off upon the tiles. Hot blood spattered on Heywood's cheek. Half blinded, but not daring to move, he saw the knife withdrawn, and a huge goblet held out to catch the flow. Then arms, goblet, and convulsive wings jerked out of sight, and the shutter slid home.

"Twice they've not seen me," thought Heywood. It was darker, here, than he had hoped. He rose more boldly to the peep-hole.

Under the arch of swords, the new recruits, now standing upright, stretched one by one their wrists over the goblet. The Incense Master pricked each yellow arm, to mingle human blood with the blood of the white cock; then, from a brazen vessel, filled the goblet to the brim. It passed from hand to hand, like a loving-cup. Each novice raised it, chanted some formula, and drank. Then all dispersed. There fell a silence.

Suddenly, in the pale face of the black image seated before the shrine, the eyes turned, scanning the company with a cold contempt. The lips moved. The voice, level and ironic, was that of Fang, the Sword-Pen:--

"O Fragrant Ones, when shall the foreign monsters perish like this cock?"

A man in black, with a red wand, bowed and answered harshly:--

"The time, Great Elder Brother, draws at hand."

"How shall we know the hour?"

"The hour," replied the Red Wand, "shall be when the Black Dog barks."

"And the day?"

Heywood pressed his ear against the chink, and listened, his five senses fused into one.

No answer came, but presently a rapid, steady clicking, strangely familiar and commonplace. He peered in again. The Red Wand stood by the abacus, rattling the brown beads with flying fingers, like a shroff. Plainly, it was no real calculation, but a ceremony before the answer. The listener clapped his ear to the crevice. Would that answer, he wondered, be a month, a week, to-morrow?

The shutter banged, the light streamed, down went Heywood against the plaster. Thick dregs from the goblet splashed on the tiles. A head, the flattened profile of the brisk man in yellow, leaned far out from the little port-hole. Grunting, he shook the inverted cup, let it dangle from his hands, stared up aimlessly at the stars, and then--to Heywood's consternation--dropped his head to meditate, looking straight down.

"He sees me," thought Heywood, and held himself ready, trembling. But the fellow made no sign, the broad squat features no change. The pose was that of vague, comfortable thought. Yet his vision seemed to rest, true as a plumb-line, on the hiding-place. Was he in doubt?--he could reach down lazily, and feel.

Worst of all, the greenish pallor in the eastern sky had imperceptibly turned brighter; and now the ribbed edge of a roof, across the way, began to glow like incandescent silver. The moon was crawling up.

The head and the dangling goblet were slowly pulled in, just before the moonlight, soft and sullen through the brown haze of the heat, stole down the wall and spread upon the tiles. The shutter remained open. But Heywood drew a free breath: those eyes had been staring into vacancy.

"Now, then," he thought, and sat up to the cranny; for the rattle of the abacus had stopped.

"The counting is complete," announced the Red Wand slowly, "the hours are numbered. The day--"

Movement, shadow, or nameless instinct, made the listener glance upward swiftly. He caught the gleam of yellow silk, the poise and downward jab, and with a great heave of muscles went shooting down the slippery channel of the cock's blood. A spearhead grazed his scalp, and smashed a tile behind him. As he rolled over the edge, the spear itself whizzed by him into the dark.

"The chap saw," he thought, in mid-air; "beastly clever--all the time--"

He landed on the spear-shaft, in a pile of dry rubbish, snatched up the weapon, and ran, dimly conscious of a quiet scurrying behind and above him, of silent men tumbling after, and doors flung violently open.

He raced blindly, but whipped about the next corner, leaving the moon at his back. Westward, somebody had told him, to the gate where dragons met.

There had been no uproar; but running his hardest down the empty corridors of the streets, he felt that the pack was gaining. Ahead loomed something gray, a wall, the end of a blind alley. Scale it, or make a stand at the foot,--he debated, racing. Before the decision came, a man popped out of the darkness.Heywood shifted his grip, drew back the spear, but found the stranger bounding lightly alongside, and muttering,--

"To the west-south, quick! A brother waits. I fool those who follow--"

Obeying, Heywood dove to the left into the black slit of an alley, while the other fugitive pattered straight on into the seeming trap, with a yelp of encouragement to the band who swept after. The alley was too dark for speed. Heywood ran on, fell, rose and ran, fell again, losing his spear. A pair of trembling hands eagerly helped him to his feet.

"My cozin's boy, he ron quick," said Wutzler. "Dose fellows, dey not catch him! Kom."

They threaded the gloom swiftly. Wutzler, ready and certain of his ground, led the tortuous way through narrow and greasy galleries, along the side of a wall, and at last through an unlighted gate, free of the town.

In the moonlight he stared at his companion, cackled, clapped his thighs, and bent double in unholy convulsions.

"My gracious me!" He laughed immoderately. "Oh, I wait zo fearful, you kom zo fonny!" For a while he clung, shaking, to the young man's arm. "My friendt, zo fonny you look! My gootness me!" At last he regained himself, stood quiet, and added very pointedly, "What did *yow* lern?"

"Nothing," replied Heywood, angrily. "Nothing. Fragrant Ones! Not a bad name. Phew!--Oh, I say, what did they mean? What Black Dog is to bark?"

"Black Dog? Black Dog iss cannon." The man became, once more, as keen as a gossip. "What cannon? When dey shoot him off?"

"Can't tell," said his friend. "That's to be their signal."

"I do not know," The conical hat wagged sagely. "I go find out." He pointed across the moonlit spaces. "Ofer dere iss your house. You can no more. *Schlafen Sie wohl.*"

The two men wrung each other's hands.

"Shan't forget this, Wutz."

"Oh, for me--all you haf done--" The outcast turned away, shaking his head sadly.

Never did Heywood's fat water-jar glisten more welcome than when he gained the vaulted bath-room. He ripped off his blood-stained clothes, scrubbed the sacrificial clots from his hair, and splashed the cool water luxuriously over his exhausted body. When at last he had thrown a kimono about him, and wearily climbed the stairs, he was surprised to see Rudolph, in the white-washed room ahead, pacing the floor and ardently twisting his little moustache. As Heywood entered, he wheeled, stared long and solemnly.

"I must wait to tell you." He stalked forward, and with his

sound left hand grasped Heywood's right. "This afternoon, you--"

"My dear boy, it's too hot. No speeches."

But Rudolph's emotion would not be hindered.

"This afternoon," he persisted, with tragic voice and eyes, "this afternoon I nearly was killed."

"So was I.--Which seems to meet that." And Heywood pulled free.

"Oh," cried Rudolph, fervently. "I know! I feel--If you knew what I--My life--"

The weary stoic in the blue kimono eyed him very coldly, then plucked him by the sleeve.--"Come here, for a bit."

Both men leaned from the window into the hot, airless night. A Chinese rebeck wailed, monotonous and nasal. Heywood pointed at the moon, which now hung clearly above the copper haze.

"What do you see there?" he asked dryly.

"The moon," replied his friend, wondering.

"Good.--You know, I was afraid you might just see Rudie Hackh."

The rebeck wailed a long complaint before he added:--

"If I didn't like you fairly well--The point is--Good old Cynthia! That bally orb may not see one of us to-morrow night, next week, next quarter. 'Through this same Garden, and for us in vain.' Every man Jack. Let me explain. It will make you better company."

CHAPTER XII

THE WAR BOARD

"Rigmarole?" drawled Heywood, and abstained from glancing at Chantel. "Dare say. However, Gilly, their rigmarole *may* mean business. On that supposition, I made my notes urgent to you chaps."

"Quite right," said Mr. Forrester, tugging his gray moustache, and studying the floor. "Obviously. Rigmarole or not, your plan is thoroughly sound: stock one house, and if the pinch comes, fortify."

Chantel drummed on Heywood's long table, and smiled quaintly, with eyes which roved out at window, and from mast to bare mast of the few small junks that lay moored against the distant bank. He bore himself, to-day, like a lazy cock of the walk. The rest of the council, Nesbit, Teppich, Sturgeon, Kempner, and the great snow-headed padre, surrounded the table with heat-worn, thoughtful faces. When they looked up, their eyes went straight to Heywood at the head; so that, though deferring to his elders, the youngest man plainly presided.

Chantel turned suddenly, merrily, his teeth flashing in a laugh.

"If we are then afraid, let us all take a jonc down the river," he scoffed, "or the next vessel for Hongkong!"

Gilly's tired, honest eyes saw only the plain statement.

"Impossible." He shook his bullet head. "We can't run away from a rumor, you know. Can we, now? The women, perhaps. But we should lose face no end--horribly."

"Let's come to facts," urged Heywood. "Arms, for example. What have we? To my knowledge, one pair of good rifles, mine and Sturgeon's. Ammunition--uncertain, but limited. Two revolvers: my Webley.450, and that little thing of Nesbit's, which is not man-stopping. Shot-guns? Every one but you, padre: fit only for spring snipe, anyway, or bamboo partridge. Hackh has just taken over, from this house, the only real weapons in the settlement--one dozen old

Mausers, Argentine, calibre .765. My predecessor left 'em, and three cases of cartridges. I've kept the guns oiled, and will warrant the lot sound.--Now, who'll lend me spare coolies, and stuff for sand-bags?"

"Over where?" puffed Sturgeon. "Where's he taking your Mausers?"

"Nunnery, of course."

"Oh, I say!" Mr. Forrester looked up, with an injured air. "As the senior here, except Dr. Earle, I naturally thought the choice would be my house."

"Right!" cried two or three voices from the foot of the table. "It should be--Farthest off--"

All talked at once, except Chantel, who eyed them leniently, and smiled as at so many absurd children. Kempner--a pale, dogged man, with a pompous white moustache which pouted and bristled while he spoke--rose and delivered a pointless oration. "Ignoring race and creed," he droned, "we must stand together--"

Heywood balanced a pencil, twirled it, and at last took to drawing. On the polished wood he scratched, with great pains, the effigy of a pig, whose snout blared forth a gale of quarter-notes.

"Whistle away!" he muttered; then resumed, as if no one had interrupted: "Very good of you, Gilly. But with your permission, I see five points.--Here's a rough sketch, made some time ago."

He tossed on the table a sheet of paper. Forrester spread it, frowning, while the others leaned across or craned over his chair.

"All out of whack, you see," explained the draughtsman; "but here are my points, Gilly. One: your house lies quite inland, with four sides to defend: the river and marsh give Rudie's but two and a fraction. Boats? Not hardly: we'd soon stop that, as you'll see, if they dare. Anyhow,--point two,--your house is all hillocks behind, and shops roundabout: here's just one low ridge, and the rest clear field. Third: the Portuguese built a well of sorts in the courtyard; water's deadly, I dare say, but your place has no well whatever. And as to four, suppose--in a sudden alarm, say, those cut off by land could run another half-chance to reach the place by river.--By the way, the nunnery has a bell to ring."

Gilbert Forrester shoved the map along to his neighbor, and cleared his throat.

"Gentlemen," he declared slowly, "you once did me the honor to say that in--in a certain event, you would consider me as acting head. Frankly, I confess, my plans were quite--ah!--vague. I wish to--briefly, to resign, in favor of this young--ah--bachelor."

"Don't go rotting me," complained Heywood, and his sallow cheeks turned ruddy. "I merely bring up these points. And five is this: your compound's very cramped, where the nunnery could shelter the goodly blooming fellowship of native converts."

Chantel laughed heartily, and stretched his legs at ease under the table.

PORTUGUESE NUNNERY:— SKETCH MAP

Marsh

I
N ← → S
W

Wall

Orange Trees

Water Gate

Chap-el

Nunnery

Well

Land Gate

Court

River

Rising Ground

Path and Field

Servant Lines

Pony Sheds

Lane

Matting Go-down

No Scale.— M. H.

"What strategy!" he chuckled, preening his moustache. "Your mythical siege--it will be brief! For me, I vote no to that: no rice-Christians filling their bellies--eating us into a surrender!" He made a pantomime of chop-sticks. "A compound full, eating, eating!"

One or two nodded, approving the retort. Heywood, slightly lifting his chin, stared at the speaker coldly, down the length of their council-board. The red in his cheeks burned darker.

"Our everlasting shame, then," he replied quietly. "It will be everlasting, if we leave these poor devils in the lurch, after cutting them loose from their people. Excuse me, padre, but it's no time to mince our words. We made them strangers in their own land. Desert 'em? Damned if we do!"

No one made reply. The padre, who had looked up, looked down quickly, musing, and smoothed his white hair with big fingers that somewhat trembled.

"Besides," continued the speaker, in a tone of apology, "we'll need 'em to man the works. Meantime, you chaps must lend coolies, eh? Look here." With rising spirits, he traced an eager finger along the map. "I must run a good strong bamboo scaffold along the inside wall, with plenty of sand-bags ready for loopholing--specially atop the servants' quarters and pony-shed, and in that northeast angle, where we'll throw up a mound or platform.--What do you say? Suggestions, please!"

Chantel, humming a tune, reached for his helmet, and rose. He paused, struck a match, and in an empty glass, shielding the flame against the breeze of the punkah, lighted a cigarette.

"Since we have appointed our dictator," he began amiably, "we may repose--"

From the landing, without, a coolie bawled impudently for the master of the house.

"Wutzler!" said Heywood, jumping up. "I mean--his messenger."

He was gone a noticeable time, but came back smiling.

"Good news, Gilly." He held aloft a scrap of Chinese paper, scrawled on with pencil. "We need expect nothing these ten days. They wait for more ammunition--'more shoots,' the text has it. The Hak Kaú--their Black Dog--is a bronze cannon, nine feet long, cast at Rotterdam in 1607. He writes, 'I saw it in shed last night, but is gone to-day. O.W.' Gentlemen, for a timid man, our friend does not scamp his reports. Thorough, rather? Little O.W. is O.K."

Chantel, still humming, had moved toward the door. All at once he halted, and stared from the landward window. Cymbals clashed somewhere below.

"What's this?" he cried sharply. The noise drew nearer, more brazen, and with it a clatter of hoofs. "Here come swordsmen!"

"To play with you, I suppose. Your fame has spread."
Heywood spoke with a slow, mischievous drawl; but he
crossed the room quickly. "What's up?"

Below, by the open gate, a gay grotesque rider reined in a
piebald pony, and leaning down, handed to the house-boy a
ribbon of scarlet paper. Behind him, to the clash of cymbals,
a file of men in motley robes swaggered into position,
wheeled, and formed the ragged front of a Falstaff regiment.
Overcome by the scarlet ribbon, the long-coated "boy"
bowed, just as through the gate, like a top-heavy boat swept
under an arch, came heaving an unwieldy screened chair,
borne by four broad men: not naked and glistening coolies,
but "Tail-less Horses" in proud livery. Before they could
lower their shafts, Heywood ran clattering down the stairs.

Slowly, cautiously, like a little fat old woman, there
clambered out from the broadcloth box a rotund man, in
flowing silks, and a conical, tasseled hat of fine straw. He
waddled down the compound path, shading with his fan a
shrewd, bland face, thoughtful, yet smooth as a babe's.

The watchers in the upper room saw Heywood greet him
with extreme ceremony, and heard the murmur of "Pray
you, I pray you," as with endless bows and deprecations the
two men passed from sight, within the house. A long time
dragged by. The visitor did not join the company, but from
another room, now and then, sounded his clear-pitched
voice, full of odd and courteous modulations. When at last
the conference ended, and their unmated footsteps crossed
the landing, a few sentences echoed from the stairway.

"That is all," declared the voice, pleasantly. "The Chow
Ceremonial says, 'That man is unwise who knowingly
throws away precious things.' And in the Analects we read,
'There is merit in dispatch.'"

Heywood's reply was lost, except the words, "stupid
people."

"In every nation," agreed the placid voice. "It is true. What
says the Viceroy of Hupeh: 'They see a charge of bird-shot,
and think they are tasting broiled owl.'--Walk slowly!"

"A safe walk, Your Excellency."

The cymbals struck up, the cavalcade, headed by ragamuffin lictors with whips, went swaying past the gate. Heywood, when he returned, was grinning.

"Wonderful old chap!" he exclaimed. "Hates this station, I fancy, much as we hate it."

"Anything to concern us?" asked Gilly.

"Intimated he could beat me at chess," laughed the young man, "and will bet me a jar of peach wine to a box of Manila cigars!"

Chantel, from a derisive dumb-show near the window, had turned to waddle solemnly down the room. At sight of Heywood's face he stopped guiltily.

"Chantel!" All the laughter was gone from the voice and the hard gray eyes. "Yesterday we humored you tin-soldier fashion, but to-day let's put away childish things.--I like that magistrate, plainly, a damned deal better than I like you. When you or I show one half his ability, we're free to mock him--in my house."

For the first time within the memory of any man present, the mimic wilted.

"I--I did not know," he stammered, "that old man was your friend." Very quiet, and a little flushed, he took his seat among the others.

"I like him no end." Still more quiet, Heywood appealed to the company. "Part for his hard luck--stuck down, a three-year term, in this neglected hole. Enemies in power, higher up. Fang, the Sword-Pen, in great favor up there.--What? Oh, said nothing directly, of course. Friendly call, and all that. But his indirections speak straight enough. We understood each other. The dregs of the town are all stirred up--bottomside topside--danger point. He, in case--you know--can't give us any help. No means, no recourse. His chief's fairly itching to cashier him.--Spoke highly of your hospital work, padre, but said, 'Even good deeds may be misconstrued.'--In short, gentlemen, without saying a word, he tells us honestly in plain terms, 'Sorry, but look out for yourselves.'"

A beggar rattled his bowl of cash in the road, below; from up the river sounded wailing cries.

"Did he mention," said the big padre, presently, "the case against my man, Chok Chung?"

Heywood's eyes became evasive, his words reluctant.

"The magistrate dodged that--that unpleasant subject. The case was forced on him. Some understrapper tried it. Let's be fair."

Dr. Earle's great elbows left the board. Without rising, he seemed to grow in bulk and stature, and send his vision past the company, into those things which are not, to confound the things which are.

"For myself, it does not matter. 'He buries His workmen, but carries on His work.'" The man spoke in a heavy, broken voice, as though it were his body that suffered. "But it comes hard to hear, from a young man, so good a friend, after many years"--The deep-set eyes returned, and with a sudden lustre, made a sharp survey from face to face. "If I have made my flock a remnant--aliens--rejected--tell me, what shall I do? Tell me. I have shut eyes and conscience, and never meddled, never!--not even when money was levied for the village idols. And here's a man beaten, cast into prison--"

He shoved both fists out on the table, and bowed his white head.

"My safety is nothing. But yours--and his.--To keep one, I desert the other. Either way." The padre groaned. "What must I choose?"

"We're all quite helpless," said Heywood, gently. "Quite. It's a long way to the nearest gunboat."

"Tell me," repeated the other, stubbornly.

At the same moment it happened that the cries came louder along the river-bank, and that some one bounded up the stairs.

The runner was Rudolph. All morning he had gone about his errands very calmly, playing the man of action, in a new philosophy learned overnight. But now he forgot to imitate his teacher, and darted in, so headlong that all the dogs came with him, bouncing and barking.

"Look," he called, stumbling toward the farther window, while Flounce the terrier and a wonk puppy ran nipping at his heels. "Come, look at them! Out on the river!"

CHAPTER XIII

THE SPARE MAN

Beyond the scant greenery of Heywood's garden--a ropy little banyan, a low rank of glossy whampee leaves, and the dusty sage-green tops of stunted olives--glared the river. Wide, savage sunlight lay so hot upon it, that to aching eyes the water shone solid, like a broad road of yellow clay. Only close at hand and by an effort of vision, appeared the tiny, quiet lines of the irresistible flood pouring toward the sea; there whipped into the pool of banyan shade black snippets and tails of reflection, darting ceaselessly after each other like a shoal of frightened minnows. But elsewhere the river lay golden, solid, and painfully bright. Things afloat, in the slumberous procession of all Eastern rivers, swam downward imperceptibly, now blurred, now outlined in corrosive sharpness.

The white men stood crowding along the spacious window. The dogs barked outrageously; but at last above their din floated, as before, the high wailing cries. A heaping cairn of round-bellied, rosy-pink earthen jars came steering past, poled by a naked statue of new copper, who balanced precariously on the edge of his hidden raft. No sound came from him; nor from the funeral barge which floated next, where still figures in white robes guarded the vermilion drapery of a bier, decked with vivid green boughs. All these were silent.

"No, above!" cried Rudolph, pointing.

After the mourners' barge, at some distance, came hurrying a boat crowded with shining yellow bodies and dull blue jackets. Long bamboo poles plied bumping along her gunwale, sticking into the air all about her, many and loose and incoordinate, like the ribs of an unfinished basket. From the bow spurted a white puff of smoke. The dull report of a musket lagged across the water.

The bullet skipped like a schoolboy's pebble, ripping out little rags of white along that surface of liquid clay.

The line of fire thus revealed, revealed the mark.

Untouched, a black head bobbed vigorously in the water, some few yards before the boat. The saffron crew, poling faster, yelled and cackled at so clean a miss, while a coolie in the bow reloaded his matchlock.

The fugitive head labored like that of a man not used to swimming, and desperately spent. It now gave a quick twist, and showed a distorted face, almost of the same color with the water.

The mouth gaped black in a sputtering cry, then closed choking, squirted out water, and gaped once more, to wail clearly:--

"I am Jesus Christ!"

In the broad, bare daylight of the river, this lonely and sudden blasphemy came as though a person in a dream might declare himself to a waking audience of skeptics. The cry, sharp with forlorn hope, rang like an appeal.

"Why--look," stammered Heywood. "He sees us--heading here. Look, it's--Quick! let me out!"

Just as he turned to elbow through his companions, and just as the cry sounded again, the matchlock blazed from the bow. No bullet skipped. The swimmer, who had reached the shallows, suddenly rose with an incredible heave, like a leaping salmon, flung one bent arm up and back in the gesture of the Laocoön, and pitched forward with a turbid splash. The quivering darkness under the banyan blotted everything: death had dispersed the black minnows there, in oozy wriggles of shadow; but next moment the fish-tail stripes chased in a more lively shoal. The gleaming potter, below his rosy cairn, stared. The mourners forgot their grief.

Heywood, after his impulse of rescue, stood very quiet.

"You saw," he repeated dully. "You all saw."

The clutching figure, bolt upright in the soaked remnant of prison rags, had in that leap and fall shown himself for Chok Chung, the Christian. He had sunk in mystery, to become at one forever with the drunken cormorant-fisher.

Obscene delight raged in the crowded boat, with yells and laughter, and flourish of bamboo poles.

"Come away from the window," said Heywood; and then to
the white-haired doctor: "Your question's answered, padre.
Strange, to come so quick." He jerked his thumb back
toward the river. "And that's only first blood."

The others had broken into wrangling.

"Escaped? Nonsense--Cat--and--mouse game, I tell you;
those devils let him go merely to--We'll never know--Of
course! Plain as your nose--To stand by, and never lift a
hand! Oh, it's--Rot! Look here, why--Acquitted, then set on
him--But we'll *never* know!--Fang watching on the spot.
Trust him!"

A calm "boy," in sky-blue gown, stood beside them, ready to
speak. The dispute paused, while they turned for his
message. It was a disappointing trifle: Mrs. Forrester waited
below for her husband, to walk home.

"Can't leave now," snapped Gilly. "I'll be along, tell her--"

"Had she better go alone?" suggested Heywood.

"No; right you are." The other swept a fretful eye about the
company. "But this business begins to look urgent.--Here,
somebody we can spare. You go, Hackh, there's a good
chap."

Chantel dropped the helmet he had caught up. Bowing
stiffly, Rudolph marched across the room and down the
stairs. His face, pale at the late spectacle, had grown red and
sulky, "Can spare me, can you?--I'm the one." He
descended, muttering.

Viewing himself thus, morosely, as rejected of men, he
reached the compound gate to fare no better with the
woman. She stood waiting in the shadow of the wall; and as
he drew unwillingly near, the sight of her--to his shame and
quick dismay--made his heart leap in welcome. She wore the
coolest and severest white, but at her throat the same small
furbelow, every line of which he had known aboard ship, in
the days of his first exile and of his recent youth. It was now
as though that youth came flooding back to greet her.

"Good-morning." He forgot everything, except that for a
few priceless moments they would be walking side by side.

She faced him with a start, never so young and beautiful as

now--her blue eyes wide, scornful, and blazing, her cheeks red and lips trembling, like a child ready to cry.

"I did not want *you*" she said curtly.

"Nor did they." Pride forged the retort for him, at a blow. He explained in the barest of terms, while she eyed him steadily, with every sign of rising temper.

"I can spare you, too," she whipped out; then turned to walk away, holding her helmet erect, in the poise of a young goddess, pert but warlike.

This double injustice left Rudolph chafing. In two strides, however, he had overtaken her.

"I am under orders," he stated grimly.

Her pace gradually slackened in the growing heat; but she went forward with her eyes fixed on the littered, sunken flags of their path. This rankling silence seemed to him more unaccountable and deadly than all former mischances, and left him far more alone. From the sultry tops of bamboos, drooping like plants in an oven, an amorous multitude of cicadas maintained the buzzing torment of steel on emery wheels, as though the universal heat had chafed and fretted itself into a dry, feverish utterance. Once Mrs. Forrester looked about, quick and angry, like one ready to choke that endless voice. But for the rest, the two strange companions moved steadily onward.

In an alley of checkered light a buffalo with a wicker nose-ring, and heavy, sagging horns that seemed to jerk his head back in agony, heaved toward them, ridden by a naked yellow infant in a nest-like saddle of green fodder. Scenting with fright the disgusting presence of white aliens, the sleep-walking monster shied, opened his eyes, and lowered his blue muzzle as if to charge. There was a pause, full of menace.

"Don't run!" said Rudolph, and catching the woman roughly about the shoulders, thrust her behind him. She clutched him tightly by the wounded arm.

The buffalo stared irresolute, with evil eyes. The naked boy in the green nest brushed a swarm of flies from his handful of sticky sweetmeats, looked up, pounded the clumsy shoulders, and shrilled a command. Staring doubtfully, and trembling, the buffalo swayed past, the wrinkled armor of his gray hide plastered with dry mud as with yellow ochre. To the slow click of hoofs, the surly monster, guided by a little child, went swinging down the pastoral shade,--ancient yet living shapes from a picture immemorial in art and poetry.

"Please," begged Rudolph, trying with his left hand to loosen her grip. "Please, that hurts."

For a second they stood close, their fingers interlacing. With a touch of contempt, he found that she still trembled, and drew short breath. Her eyes slowly gathered his meaning.

"Oh, that!" She tore her hand loose, as though burned. "That! It *was* all true, then. I forgot."

She caught aside her skirts angrily, and started forward in all her former disdain. But this, after their brief alliance, was not to be tolerated.

"What was all true?" he insisted. "You shall not treat me so. If anybody has a right--"

After several paces, she flashed about at him in a whirl of words:--

"All alike, every one of you! And I was fool enough to think you were different!" The conflict in her eyes showed real, beyond suspicion. "He told me all about it. Last evening. And you dare talk of rights, and come following me here--"

"Lucky I did," retorted Rudolph, with sudden spirit; and holding out his wounded arm, indignantly: "That scratch, if you know how it came--"

"I know, perfectly." She stared as at some crowning impudence. "He was chicken-hearted. You came off cheaply.--I know all you said. But the one thing I'll never understand, is where you found the courage, after he struck you, at the club. You'll always have *that* to admire!"

"After he struck"--A light broke in on Rudolph, somehow. "Chantel? Oh, that liar!"

He wheeled and started to go back.

"Wait, stop!" she called, in a strangely altered voice, which

brought him up short. "They're all with him now. You can't-
-What did you mean?"

He explained, sulkily at first, but ending in a kind of
generous rage. "So I couldn't even stand up to him. And
except for Maurice Heywood--Oh, you need not frown; he's
the best friend I ever had."

Mrs. Forrester had walked on, with the same cloudy aspect,
the same light, impatient step. He felt the greater surprise
when, suddenly turning, she raised toward him her odd,
enticing, pointed face, and the friendly mischief of her eyes.

"The best?" she echoed, in the same half-whisper as when
she had flattered him, that afternoon in the dusky well of
the pagoda stairway. "The very best friend? Don't you think
you have a better?"

Rudolph stared.

"Oh, you funny, funny boy!" she cried, with a bewildering
laugh, of delight and pride. "I hate people all prim and
circumspect, and you--You'd have flown back there straight
at him, before my--before all the others. That's why I like
you so!--But you must leave that horrid, lying fellow to me."

All unaware, she had led him along the blinding white wall
of the Forrester compound, and halted in the hot shadow
that lay under the tiled gateway. As though timidly, her hand
stole up and rested on his forearm.

"So sorry." The confined space, narrow and covered, gave
to her voice a plaintive ring. "That's twice you protected me,
and I hurt you.--You *are* different. This doesn't happen
between people, often. When you did--that, for me,
yesterday, didn't it seem different and rather splendid, and--
like a book?"

"It seemed nonsense," replied Rudolph, sturdily. "The heat.
We were fools."

She laughed again, and at close range watched him from
under consciously drooping lashes that almost veiled a liquid
brilliancy. Everywhere the cicadas kept the heat vibrating
with their strident buzz. It recalled some other widespread
mist of treble music, long ago. The trilling of frogs, that had
been, before.

"You dear, brave boy," she said slowly. "You're so honest, too. I'm not ungrateful. Do you know what I'd like--Oh, there's the *amah!*"

She drew back, with an impatient gesture.

"That stupid, fat Mrs. Earle's waiting for me.--I hate to leave you." The stealthy brightness of her admiration changed to a slow, inscrutable appeal. "Don't forget. Haven't you--a better friend?" And with an instant, bold, and tantalizing grimace, she had vanished within.

To his homeward march, her cicadas shrilled the music of fifes. He, the despised, the man to spare, now cocked up his helmet like fortune's minion, dizzy with new honors. Nobody had ever praised him to his face. And now she, she of all the world, had spoken words which he feared and longed to believe, and which even said still less than her searching and mysterious look.

On the top of his exultation, he reached the nunnery, and entered his big, bare living-room, to find Heywood stretched in a wicker chair.

"Hallo, Rudie! I've asked myself to tiffin," drawled the lounger, from a little tempest of blue smoke, tossed by the punkah. "How's the fair Bertha?--Mausers all right? And by the way, did you make that inventory of provisions?"

Rudolph faced him with a sudden conviction of guilt, of treachery to a leader.

"Yes," he stammered; "I--I'll get it for you."

He passed into his bedroom, caught up the written list from a table, and for a moment stood as if dreaming. Before him the Mausers, polished and orderly, shone in their new rack against the lime-coated wall. Though appearing to scan them, Rudolph saw nothing but his inward confusion. "After all this man did for me," he mused. What had loosed the bond, swept away all the effects?

A sound near the window made him turn. An imp in white and red livery, Pêng, the little billiard-marker from the club, stood hurling things violently into the outer glare.

"What thing you do?" called Rudolph, sharply.

Some small but heavy object clattered on the floor. The urchin stooped, snatched it up, and flung it hurtling clean over the garden to the river. He turned, grinning amiably. "Goo-moh? ning-seh. How too you too," he chanted. "I am welly? glat to-see you." A boat-coolie, he explained, had called this house bad names. He, Pêng, threw stones. Bad man.

"Out of here, you rascal!" Rudolph flicked a riding-whip at the scampering legs, as the small defender of his honor bolted for the stairs.

"What's wrong?"

Heywood appeared promptly at the door.

From the road, below, a gleeful voice piped:--

"Goat-men! Baby-killers!"

In the noon blaze, Pêng skipped derisively, jeered at them, performed a brief but indecorous pantomime, and then, kicking up his heels with joy, scurried for his life.

"Chucked his billet," said Heywood, without surprise. "Little devil, I always thought--What's missing?"

Rudolph scanned his meagre belongings, rummaged his dressing-table, opened a wardrobe.

"Nothing," he answered. "A boat-coolie--"

But Heywood had darted to the rack of Mausers, knelt, and sprung up, raging.

"Side-bolts! Man," he cried, in a voice that made Rudolph jump,--"man, why didn't you stop him? The side-bolts, all but two.--Young heathen, he's crippled us: one pair of rifles left."

CHAPTER XIV

OFF DUTY

The last of the sunlight streamed level through a gap in the western ridges. It melted, with sinuous, tender shadows, the dry contour of field and knoll, and poured over all the parching land a liquid, undulating grace. Like the shadow of clouds on ripe corn, the red tiles of the village roofs patched the countryside. From the distant sea had come a breath of air, cool enough to be felt with gratitude, yet so faint as neither to disturb the dry pulsation of myriad insect-voices, nor to blur the square mirrors of distant rice-fields, still tropically blue or icy with reflected clouds.

Miss Drake paused on the knoll, and looked about her.

"This remains the same, doesn't it, for all our troubles?" she said; then to herself, slowly, "'It is a beauteous evening, calm and free.'"

Heywood made no pretense of following her look.

"'Dear Nun,'" he blurted; "no, how does it go again?--'dear child, that walkest with me here--'"

The girl started down the slope, with the impatience of one whose mood is frustrated. The climate had robbed her cheeks of much color, but not, it seemed, of all.

"Your fault," said Heywood, impenitent. "Merely to show you. I could quote, once."

"Aged Man!" She laughed, as though glad of this turn. "I like you better in prose. Go on, please, where we left off. What did you do then?"

Heywood's smile, half earnest, half mischievous, obediently faded.

"Oh, that! Why, then, of course, I discharged Rudolph's gatekeeper, put a trusty of my own in his place, sent out to hire a diver, and turned all hands to hunting. 'Obviously,' as Gilly would say.--We picked up two side-bolts in the garden, by the wall, one in the mud outside, and three the diver got in shallow water. Total recovered, six; plus two Pêng had no time for, eight. We can ill spare four guns, though; and the affair shows they keep a beastly close watch."

"Yes," said Miss Drake, absently; then drew a slow breath. "Pêng was the most promising pupil we had."

"He was," stated her companion, "a little, unmitigated, skipping, orange-tawny goblin!"

She made no reply. As they footed slowly along the winding path, Flounce, the fox-terrier, who had scouted among strange clumps of bamboo, now rejoined them briskly, cantering with her fore-legs delicately stiff and joyful. Miss Drake stooped to pat her, saying:--

"Poor little dog. Little Foreign Dog!" She rose with a sigh, to add incongruously, "Oh, the things we dream beforehand, and then the things that happen!"

"I don't know." Heywood looked at her keenly. "Sometimes they're the same."

The jealous terrier scored her dusty paws down his white drill, from knee to ankle, before he added:--

"You know how the Queen of Heaven won her divinity."

"Another," said the girl, "of your heathen stories?"

"Rather a pretty one," he retorted. "It happened in a seaport, a good many hundred miles up the coast. A poor girl lived there, with her mother, in a hut. One night a great gale blew, so that everybody was anxious. Three junks were out somewhere at sea, in that storm. The girl lay there in the dark. Her sweetheart on board, it would be in a Western story; but these were only her friends, and kin, and townsmen, that were at stake. So she lay there in the hut, you see, and couldn't rest. And then it seemed to her, in the dark, that she was swimming out through the storm, out and out, and not in the least afraid. She had become larger, and more powerful, somehow, than the rain, or the dark, or the whole ocean; for when she came upon the junks tossing there, she took one in each hand, the third in her mouth, and began to swim for home. Just retrieved 'em, you know. But then across the storm she heard her mother calling in the dark, and had to open her mouth to answer. So she lost that junk."

"Well, then her spirit was back in the hut. But next day the two junks came in; the third one, never. And for that dream, she was made, after her death, the great and merciful Queen of Heaven."

As Heywood ended, they were entering a pastoral village, near the town, but hidden low under great trees, ancient and widely gnarled.

"You told that," said Miss Drake, "as though it had really happened."

"If you believe, these things have reality; if not, they have none." His gesture, as he repeated the native maxim, committed him to neither side.

Miss Drake looked back toward the hills.

"Her dream was play, compared to--some."

"That," he answered, "is abominably true."

The curt, significant tone made her glance at him quickly. In her dark eyes there was no impatience, but only trouble.

"We do better," she said, "when we are both busy."

He nodded, as though reluctantly agreeing, not so much to the words as to the silence which followed.

The evening peace, which lay on the fields and hills, had flooded even the village streets. Without pause, without haste, the endless labor of the day went on as quiet as a summer cloud. Meeting or overtaking, coolies passed in single file, their bare feet slapping the enormous flags of antique, sunken granite, their twin baskets bobbing and creaking to the rhythm of their wincing trot. The yellow muscles rippled strongly over straining ribs, as with serious faces, and slant eyes intent on their path, they chanted in pairs the ageless refrain, the call and answer which make burdens lighter:--

"O heh!--O ha?
 O ho ho!
 O heh!--O ha?
 O ho ho!"

From hidden places sounded the whir of a jade-cutter's wheel, a cobbler's rattle, or the clanging music of a forge. Yet everywhere the slow movements, the faded, tranquil colors,--dull blue garments, dusky red tiles, deep bronze-green foliage overhanging a vista of subdued white and gray,--consorted with the spindling shadows and low-streaming vesper light. Keepers of humble shops lounged in the open air with their gossips, smoking bright pipes of the Yunnan white copper, nodding and blinking gravely. Above them, no less courteous and placid, little doorway shrines besought the Earth-God to lead the Giver of Wealth within. Sometimes, where a narrow lane gaped opposite a door, small stone lions sat grinning upon pillars, to scare away the Secret Arrow of misfortune. But these rarely: the village seemed a happy place, favored of the Influences. In the grateful coolness men came and went, buying, joking, offering neighborly advice to chance-met people.

A plump woman, who carried two tiny silver fish in an immense flat basket, grinned at Miss Drake, and pointed roguishly.

"See the two boats going by!" she called. "Her feet are bigger than my Golden Lilies!" And laughing, she wriggled her own dusty toes, strong, free, and perfect in modeling.

An old, withered barber looked up from shaving a blue forehead, under a tree.

"Their women," he growled, "are shameless, and walk everywhere!"

But a stern man, bearing a palm-leaf fan and a lark in a cage, frowned him down.

"She brought my son safe out of the Three Sicknesses," he declared. "Mind your trade, Catcher of Lively Ones!" Then bending over the cage, with solicitude, he began gently to fan the lark. As Heywood and the girl paused beside him, he glanced up, and smiled gravely. "I give my pet his airing," he said; and then, quickly but quietly, "When you reach the town, do not pass through the West Quarter. It is full of evil-minded persons. Their placards are posted."

A shrill trio of naked boys came racing and squabbling, to offer grasshoppers for sale.

"We have seen no placards," replied Heywood.

"You will to-morrow," said the owner of the lark, calmly; and squatting, became engrossed in poking a grasshopper between the brown, varnished splints of the cage. "Maker of Music, here is your evening rice."

The two companions passed on, with Flounce timidly at heel.

"You see," Heywood broke out. "Warnings everywhere. Now please, won't you listen to my advice? No telling when the next ship *will* call, but when it does--"

"I can't run away." She spoke as one clinging to a former answer. "I must stand by my dream, such as it used to be-- and even such as it is."

He eyed her sadly, shook his head, and said no more. For a moment they halted, where the path broadened on a market-place, part shade, part luminous with golden dust. A squad of lank boys, kicking miraculously with flat upturned soles, kept a wicker ball shining in the air, as true and lively as a plaything on a fountain-jet. Beyond, their tiny juniors, girls and boys knee-high, and fat tumbling babies in rainbow finery, all hand-locked and singing, turned their circle inside out and back again, in the dizzy graces of the "Water Wheel." Other boys, and girls still trousered and queued like boys, played at hopscotch, in and out among shoes that lay across the road. All traffic, even the steady trotting coolies, fetched a lenient compass roundabout.

"Lucky Hand, Lucky Hand! Allow me to pass," begged a coffin-maker's man, bent under a plank. "These Long-Life boards are heavy."

"Ho, Lame Chicken!" called another, blocked by the hop-scotch. He was a brown grass-cutter, who grinned, and fondled a smoky cloth that buzzed--some tribe of wild bees, captured far afield. "Ho, Lame Chicken! Do not bump me. They will sting."

He came through safely; for at the same moment the musical "Cling-clank" of a sweetmeat-seller's bell turned the game into a race. The way was clear, also, for a tiny, aged collector of paper, flying the gay flag of an "Exalted Literary Society," and plodding, between two great baskets, on his

pious rounds. "Revere and spare," he piped, at intervals,--
"revere and spare the Written Word!"

All the bright picture lingered with the two alien wayfarers,
long after they had passed and the sun had withdrawn from
their path. In the hoary peace of twilight,--

"What can *we* do here?" the girl cried abruptly. "There--I
never meant to say it. But it runs in my head all the time. I
work and work, to keep it down. What can we do here?"

Heywood watched her face, set straight before them, and
now more clearly cut in the failing light. Were there only
pride in those fine and resolute lines, it might have been a
face from some splendid coin, or medal of victory.

"You work too hard," he said. "Think, instead, of all the
good--"

But at that she seemed to wince.

"The good? As if there weren't dark streets and crooked
children at home! Oh, the pride and ignorance that sent me
here!" She spoke quietly, with a kind of wonder. "Just blind,
ignorant feelings, I took them for--for something too great
and mysterious. It's all very strange to look back on, and try
to put into words. I remember painted glass, and solemn
music--and thinking--then!--that I knew this lovely and
terrible world--and its Maker and Master." She looked down
the dusky lanes, where glowworm lanterns began to bob and
wink. "Oh, this land! where you see the days running into
years!"

"The Dragon's a wise old beast," he ventured. "He teaches--
something."

She assented gravely:--

"And in those days I thought it was a dark continent--of lost
souls."

"There are no dark continents," declared Heywood
suddenly, in a broken voice. "The heart of one man--can
hold more darkness--You would never see into it--"

"Don't!" she cried sharply. "What did we promise?"

They stood close in the dusk, and a tremor, a wave, passed

through them both.

"I forgot--I couldn't help"--he stammered; then, as they stumbled forward, he regained his former tone, keen and ready. "Mustn't get to fussing about our work, must we?-- Curious thing: speaking of dreams, you know. The other night I thought you were somewhere out on board a junk, and Flounce with you. I swam like anything, miles and miles, but couldn't get out to you. Worked like steam, and no headway. Flounce knew I was coming, but you didn't. Deuced odd, how real it seemed."

She laughed, as though they had walked past some danger.

"And speaking of dragons," she rejoined. "They *do* help. The man in the story, that dipped in dragon's blood, was made invulnerable."

"Oh?" He stood plainly at a loss. "Oh, I see. German, wasn't he?--Pity they didn't pop Rudie Hackh in!"

Her swift upward glance might have been admiration, if she had not said:--

"Your mind works very slowly."

"Oh?" Again he paused, as though somewhat hurt; then answered cheerfully: "Dare say. Always did. Thought at first you meant the rattan-juice kind, from Sumatra."

The gate of the town yawned black. From the streets glimmered a few lanterns, like candles in a long cave. But shunning these unfriendly corridors, he led her roundabout, now along the walls, now through the dim ways of an outlying hamlet. A prolonged shriek of growing fright and anguish came slowly toward them--the cry of a wheelbarrow carrying the great carcass of a pig, waxy white and waxy red, like an image from a chamber of horrors. In the blue twilight, fast deepening, the most familiar things became grotesque. A woman's voice telling stories behind shadow pictures, and the capricious play of the black puppets on her lighted screen, had the effect of incantation. Before the booth of a dentist, the long strings of black teeth swayed in the lantern-glow, rattling, like horrid necklaces of cannibals. And from a squat den--where on a translucent placard in the dull window flickered the words "Foreign Earth," and the guttering door-lantern hinted "As You Like It"--there came a sweet, insidious, potent smell that seemed more poisonous than mere opium.

"Let's go faster," said the girl. "Somehow, the dark makes me uneasy to-night."

Skirting the town, they struck at last the open road beyond, and saw against a fading sky the low black bulk of the nunnery, pierced with orange squares. Past its landward wall, lanterns moved slowly, clustered here and there by twos and threes, and dispersed. Cackling argument came from the ditch, wherever the lantern-bearers halted; and on the face of the wall, among elbowing shadows, shone dim strips of scarlet. Both pillars of the gate were plastered with them.

"Placards," said Heywood. "Things are ripening fast." Lighting match from match, he studied the long red scrolls, crowded with neat rows of symbols. He read them off slowly.

'The Garden of the Three Exquisites.'--Pshaw! that's a theatre notice: enterprising manager.--Ah, more like it. Long preamble, regular trimetrical platitudes--here we are:--

"'These Red-Bristled Ghosts teach their dupes to break the ancestral tablets, and to worship the picture of a naked infant, which points one finger toward heaven, another toward earth.--To each man entering the False Religion, a pill is given which confuses and darkens the mind.--Why they dig out babies' eyes: from one hundred pounds of Chinese lead can be extracted seven pounds of silver, and the remaining ninety-three pounds can be sold at the original cost. This silver can be extracted only by the elixir of black eyes. The green eyes of barbarians are of no use.'-- Really, what follows is too--er--obscure. But here's the close: 'Tao-tais of the villages, assemble your population. Patriots, join! Let us hurl back these wizard-beasts beyond the oceans, to take their place among the strange things of creation!'"

"And the big characters," she added, "the big characters you tried to hide, are 'Kill' and 'Burn'?"

Gray eyes and dark eyes met steadily, while the last match, reddening the blood in his fingers, slowly burned out

CHAPTER XV

KAU FAI

At the top of the nunnery stairs, Rudolph met them with awkward ceremony, and with that smiling air of encouragement which a nurse might use in trying cheerfully to deceive a sick man. Heywood laughed, without mercy, at this pious fraud.

"Hallo, you Red-Bristled Ghost!" he cried. "We came early-- straight from our walk. Are the rest coming? And did my cook arrive to help yours?"

Their host, carried by assault, at once became less mournful.

"The cook is here," he replied, "by the kitchen-sounds. They disagree, I think. I have asked everybody. We should have a full dinner-table."

"Good," said his friend; and then whispering, as they followed Miss Drake to the living-room, "I say, don't act as though you expected the ghost of Banquo."

In the bare, white loft, by candle-light, Sturgeon sat midway in some long and wheezy tale, to which the padre and his wife listened with true forbearance. Greetings over, the stodgy annalist continued. The story was forgotten as soon as ended; talk languished; and even by the quaking light of the candles, it was plain that the silence was no mere waiting solemnity before meat, but a period of tension.

The relief came oddly. Up from the road sounded a hubbub of voices, the tramp of feet, and loud halloos.

"By Jove!" cried Sturgeon, like a man who fears the worst; and for all his bulk, he was first at the window.

A straggling file of lanterns, borne by some small army, came jogging and crowding to a halt under the walls. Yellow faces gleamed faintly, bare heads bobbed, and men set down burdens, grunting. Among the vanguard an angry voice scolded in a strange tongue. "*Burra suar!*" it raged; then hailed imperiously, "*Ko hai?*"

Where the lanterns clustered brightest, an active little figure in white waved a helmet, crying,--

"On deck! Where the devil does MauriceHeywood live?"

"I'm up here," called that young man.

For reply, the stranger began to skip among his cohorts, jerking out his white legs like a dancing marionette. Then, with a sudden drop-kick, he sent the helmet flickering high into the darkness over the wall.

"Here we come!" he shouted, in hilarious warning. The squabbling retinue surged after him through the gate, and one by one the lanterns disappeared under the covered way.

"It's the captain!" laughed Heywood, in amazement. "Kneebone--ashore! He can't be sober!"

All stared; for Captain Kneebone, after one historically brief and outspoken visit, had never in all these years set foot in the port. The two young men hurried to the stairs.

Chinamen and lanterns crowded the courtyard, stuffed the passage, and still came straggling in at the gate. By the noise and clatter, it might have been a caravan, or a band of half-naked robbers bringing plunder. Everywhere, on the stone flags, coolies were dumping down bundles, boxes, jute-bags crammed with heavy objects. Among them, still brawling in bad Hindustani, the little captain gave his orders. At sight of Heywood, however, he began once more to caper, with extravagant grimaces. By his smooth, ruddy face, and tunic of purest white, he seemed a runaway parson gone farther wrong than ever.

"I've come to stay a month!" he cried; and dancing up, caught Heywood's hands and whirled him about. "I was fair bursting to see ye, my boy! And here we are, at last!"

Though his cheeks were flushed, and eyes alarmingly bright, he was beyond question sober. Over his head, Heywood and Rudolph exchanged an anxious glance.

"Good! but this is Hackh's house--the nunnery," said the one; and the other added, "You're just in time for dinner."

The captain found these facts to be excruciating. He clapped Rudolph on the arm, and crowed:--

"Nunnery? We'll make it a bloomin' chummery!--Dinner be 'anged! A banquet. What's more, I've brought the chow"--he swept the huddled boxes with a prodigal gesture,--"lashin's o' food and drink! That's what it is: a banquet!"

He turned again to his sweating followers, and flung the head coolie a handful of silver, crying, "*Sub-log kiswasti! Divide, and be off with ye! Jao, ye beggars!* Not a pice more. Finish! I'll not spend it all on *you*!" Then, pouncing on the nearest crate, he burst it open with a ferocious kick. "Stores? The choicest to be 'ad in all Saigong! Look here"--He held up a tin and scanned the label triumphantly: "Chow de Bruxelles, what? Never saw chow spelt with an 'x' before, did ye? French, my boy. Bad spellers, but good cooks, are the French."

Heywood lost his worried frown. Something had happened,--evidently at Calcutta, for the captain always picked up his vernacular where he dropped his latest cargo; but at all events these vagaries were not the effect of heat or loneliness.

"What's up, Captain?" he laughed.

But now that the coolies had gone, Captain Kneebone's heels were busy, staving open boxes right and left. A bottle rolled out, and smashed in a hissing froth of champagne.

"Plenty more," he cried, rejoicing. "That shows ye how much *I* care! Oho!" Suddenly he turned from this destruction, and facing Heywood, began mysteriously to exult over him. "Old fool and his earnings, eh? Fixed ideas, eh? 'No good,' says you. 'That cock won't fight,' says you. 'Let it alone.'--Ho-ho! What price fixed ideas now?"

The eyes of his young friend widened in unbelief.

"No," he cried, with a start: "you haven't?"

The captain seized both hands again, and took on--for his height--a Roman stateliness.

"I have." He nodded solemnly. "Bar sells, I have. No more, now. We'll--be-George, we'll announce it, at the banquet! Announce, that's the word. First time in *my* life: announce!"

Heywood suddenly collapsed on a sack, and laughed himself

into abject silence.

"Awfully glad, old chap," he at last contrived to say, and again choked. The captain looked down at the shaking body with a singular, benign, and fatherly smile.

"A funny world, ain't it?" he declared sagely. "I've known this boy a long time," he explained to Rudolph. "This matter's--We'll let you in, presently. Lend me some coolies here, while we turn your dinner into my banquet. Eh? You don't care? Once in a bloomin' lifetime."

With a seafaring bellow, he helped Rudolph to hail the servants' quarters. A pair of cooks, a pair of Number Twos, and all the "learn-pidgin" youngsters of two households came shuffling into the court; and arriving guests found all hands broaching cargo, in a loud confusion of orders and miscomprehension.

The captain's dinner was the more brilliant. Throughout the long, white room, in the slow breeze of the punkah, scores of candles burned soft and tremulous, as though the old days had returned when the brown sisters lighted their refectory; but never had their table seen such profusion of viands, or of talk and laughter. The Saigon stores--after daily fare--seemed of a strange and Corinthian luxury. The captain's wine proved excellent. And his ruddy little face, beaming at the head of the table, wore an extravagant, infectious grin. His quick blue eyes danced with the light of some ineffable joke. He seemed a conjurer, creating banquets for sheer mischief in the wilderness.

"There's a soup!" he had proclaimed. "Patent, mind ye! Stick a knife into the tin, and she 'eats 'erself!"

Among all the revelers, one face alone showed melancholy. Chantel, at the foot of the table, sat unregarded by all save Rudolph, who now and then caught from him a look filled with gloom and suspicion. It was beside Rudolph that Mrs. Forrester laughed and chattered, calling all eyes toward her, and yet finding private intervals in which to dart a sidelong shaft at her neighbor. Rudolph's ears shone coral pink; for now again he was aboard ship, hiding a secret at once dizzy, dangerous, and entrancing. Across the talk, the wine, the many lights, came the triumph of seeing that other hostile face, glowering in defeat. Never before had Chantel, and all the others, dwindled so far into such nonentity, or her presence vibrated so near.

Soon he became aware that Captain Kneebone had risen, with a face glowing red above the candles. Even Sturgeon forgot the flood of bounties, and looked expectantly toward their source. The captain cleared his throat, faltered, then turning sheepish all at once, hung his head.

"Be 'anged, I can't make a speech, after all," he grumbled; and wheeling suddenly on Heywood, with a peevish air of having been defrauded: "Aboard ship I could sit and think up no end o' flowery talk, and now it's all gone!"

He stared at his plate miserably. It was Miss Drake who came to his rescue.

"Tell us the secret," she begged. "How do you manage all these nice things?"

The captain's eyes surveyed the motley collection down the length of the bright table, then returned to her, gratefully:--

"This ain't anything. Only a little--bloomin'--"

"Impromptu," suggested Heywood.

"That's the word!" Captain Kneebone eyed them both with uncommon favor. "That's it, ye know. I just 'opped about Saigong like a--jackdaw, picking up these impromptus. But I came here all the way to break the news proper, by word o' mouth."

He faced the company, and gathering himself for the effort,--

"I'm rich," he declared. "I'm da--I'm remarkable rich."

Pausing for the effect, he warmed to his oratory.

"It ain't for me to boast. Sailormen as a rule are bad hands to save money. But I've won first prize in the Derby Sweepstake Lott'ry, and the money's safe to my credit at the H.K. and S. in Calcutta, and I'm retired and going Home! More money than the old Kut Sing earned since her launching--so much I was frightened, first, and lost my sleep! And me without chick nor child, as the saying is--to go Home and live luxurious ever after!"

"Ow!" cried Nesbit, "lucky beggar!"--"Sincerely glad," said Mr. Forrester. And a volley of compliments went round the board. The captain plainly took heart, and flushing still redder at so much praise and good will, stood now at ease, chuckling.

"Most men," he began, when there came a lull, "most men makes a will after they're dead. That's a shore way o' doing things! Now *I* want to see the effects, living. So be 'anged, here goes, right and proper. To Miss Drake, for her hospital and kiddies, two thousand rupees."

In the laughter and friendly uproar, the girl sat dazed.

"What shall I say?" she whispered, wavering between amusement and distress. "I can't accept it--"

"Nonsense!" grumbled Heywood, with an angry glance. "Don't spoil the happiest evening of an old man's life."

"You're right," she answered quickly; and when the plaudits ended, she thanked the captain in a very simple, pretty speech, which made him duck and grin,--a proud little benefactor.

"That ain't all," he cried gayly; then leveled a threatening finger, like a pistol, at her neighbor. "Who poked fun at me, first and last? Who always came out aboard to tell me what an old ass I was? Fixed ideas, eh? No go?--Look you here. What did I come so many hundred miles for? To say what I always said: half-shares." The light-blue eyes, keen with sea-cunning and the lonely sight of many far horizons, suffered an indescribable change. "My boy, the half's yours. There's two rich men here to-night. I've come to take you Home."

It was Heywood's turn to be struck dumb. He grew very pale.

"Oh, I say," he stammered at last, "it's not fair--"

"Don't spoil the happiest evening--" whispered the girl beside him.

He eyed her ruefully, groaned, then springing up, went swiftly to the head of the table and wrung the captain's brown paw, without a word to say.

"Can do, can do," said Captain Kneebone, curtly. "I was

afraid ye might not want to come."

Then followed a whirlwind; and Teppich rose with his moustache bristling, and the ready Nesbit jerked him down again in the opening sentence; and everybody laughed at Heywood, who sat there so white, with such large eyes; and the dinner going by on the wings of night, the melancholy "boy" circled the table, all too soon, with a new silver casket full of noble cigars from Paiacombo, Manila, and Dindigul.

As the three ladies passed the foot of the table, Rudolph saw Mrs. Forrester make an angry signal. And presently, like a prisoner going to his judge, Chantel slipped out of the room. He was not missed; for already the streaming candle-flames stood wreathed in blue layers, nor was it long before the captain, mounting his chair, held a full glass aloft.

"Here," he cried in triumph, "here's to every nail in the hoof--"

The glass crashed into splinters and froth. A flying stone struck the boom of the punkah, and thumped on the table. Through the open windows, from the road, came a wild chorus of yells, caught up and echoed by many voices in the distance.

"Shutters!" called Heywood. "Quick!"

As they slammed them home, more stones drummed on the boards and clattered against the wall. Conches brayed somewhere, followed by an unaccountable, sputtering fusillade as of tiny muskets, and then by a formidable silence. While the banqueters listened in the smoky room, there came a sullen, heavy sound, like a single stroke on a large and very slack bass-drum.

"*Kaú fai!*" shrilled the voices below; and then in a fainter gabble, as though hurrying off toward the sound,--"*kaú fai!*"

"The Black Dog," said Heywood, quietly. "He has barked. Earlier than we figured, Gilly. Lucky the scaffolding's up. Gentlemen, we all know our posts. Guns are in the first bedroom. Quietly, now. Rudie, go call Chantel. Don't frighten the women. If they ask about that noise, tell 'em anything--Dragon Boat Festival beginning. Anything.--We can easily hold this place, while the captain gets 'em out to his ship."

The captain wheeled, with an injured air.

"What ship?" he inquired testily. "Told ye, plain, I was retired. Came the last bit in a stinking native boat, and *she's* cleared by now. Think I carry ships in my pocket?"

Outside, the swollen discord of shouts, thunder of gongs, and hoarse calling of the conches came slowly nearer, extending through the darkness.

CHAPTER XVI

THE GUNWALE

Rudolph's mission began quietly, with a glimpse which he afterward recalled as incredibly peaceful. Two of the women, at least, showed no fear. In the living-room sat Mrs. Earle, her chin cramped on her high bosom, while she mournfully studied his colored picture-book of the Rhine. Miss Drake, who leaned in one of the river windows, answered him, saying rather coldly that Chantel and Mrs. Forrester had gone down to the garden.

In the court, however, he ran across Ah Pat, loitering beside a lantern. The compradore grinned, and in a tone of great unconcern called out that the pair were not in the garden. "Walkee so." He pointed down the passage to the main gate, and hooked his thumb toward the right, to indicate their course. "Makee finish, makee die now," he added calmly; "too muchee, no can."

Rudolph experienced his first shock of terror, like an icy blow on the scalp. They had gone outside before the alarm; she, Bertha, was swept away in that tumult which came raging through the darkness.--He stood transfixed, but only for an instant, rather by the stroke of helplessness than by fear; and then, blindly, without plan or foresight, darted down the covered way. The tiny flame of a pith wick, floating in a saucer of oil, showed Heywood's gatekeeper sitting at his post, like a gnome in the gallery of a mine. Rudolph tore away the bar, heard the heavy gate slam shut, and found himself running down the starlit road.

Not all starlight, however; a dim red glow began to flicker on the shapes which rushed behind him in his flight. Wheeling once, he saw two broad flames leaping high in wild and splendid rivalry,--one from Heywood's house, one from the club. He caught also a whirling impression of many heads and arms, far off, tiny, black, and crowded in rushing disorder; of pale torches in the road; and of a hissing, snarling shout, a single word, like "*Sha, sha!*" repeated incessantly in a high key. The flame at the club shot up threefold, with a crash; and a glorious criss-cross multitude of sparks flew hissing through the treetops, like fiery tadpoles through a net.

He turned and ran on, dazzled; fell over some one who lay groaning; rose on hands and knees, groped in the dust, and suddenly fingered thin, rough cloth, warm and sopping. In a nausea of relief, he felt that this was a native,--some unknown dying man, who coughed like a drunkard.

Rudolph sprang up and raced again, following by habit the path which he and she had traversed at noon. Once, with a heavy collision, he stopped short violently in the midst of crowded men, who shouted, clung to him, wrestling, and struck out with something sharp that ripped his tunic. He kicked, shook them off, hammered his fists right and left, and ran free, with a strange conviction that to-night he was invincible. Stranger still, as the bamboo leaves now and then brushed his bare forehead, he missed the sharp music of her cicadas.

The looming of a wall checked him. Here stood her house; she had the briefest possible start of him, and he had run headlong the whole way; by all the certainty of instinct, he knew that he had chosen the right path: why, then, had he not overtaken her? If she met that band which he had just broken through--He wavered in the darkness, and was turning wildly to race back, when a sudden light sprang up before him in her window. He plunged forward, in at the gate, across a plot of turf, stumbled through the Goddess of Mercy bamboo that hedged the door, and went falling up the dark stairs, crying aloud,--for the first time in his life,-- "Bertha! Bertha!"

Empty rooms rang with the name, but no one answered. At last, however, reaching the upper level, he saw by lamplight, through the open door, two figures struggling. Just before he entered, she tore herself free and went unsteadily across the room. Chantel, white and abject, turned as in panic.

"Oh!" Plainly he had not expected to see another face as white as his own. Breathless and trembling, he spoke in a strangely little voice; but his staring eyes lighted with a sudden and desperate resolution. "Help me with her," he begged. "She won't listen. The woman's out of her wits."

He caught Rudolph by the arm; and standing for a moment

like close friends, the two panting rivals watched her in stupefaction. She ransacked a great cedar chest, a table, shelves, boxes, and strewed the contents on the floor,--silk scarfs, shining Benares brass, Chinese silver, vivid sarongs from the Preanger regency, Kyoto cloisonné, a wild heap of plunder from the bazaars of all the nations where Gilly's meagre earnings had been squandered. A Cingalese box dropped and burst open, scattering bright stones, false or precious, broadcast. She trampled them in her blind and furious search.

"Come," said Chantel, and snatched at her. "Leave those. Come to the boat. Every minute--"

She pushed him aside like a thing without weight or meaning, stooped again among the gay rubbish, caught up a necklace, flung it down for the sake of a brooch, then dropped everything and turned with blank, dilated eyes, and the face of a child lost in a crowd.

"Rudolph," she whimpered, "help me. What shall I do?"

Without waiting for answer, she bent once more to sort and discard her pitiful treasures, to pause vaguely, consider, and wring her hands. Rudolph, in his turn, caught her by the arm, but fared no better.

"We must humor her," whispered Chantel, and, kneeling like a peddler among the bazaar-stuffs, spread on the floor a Java sarong, blue and brown, painted with men and buffaloes. On this he began to heap things pell-mell.

The woman surrendered, and all at once flung her arms about Rudolph, hiding her face, and clinging to him as if with the last of her strength.

"Come, he'll bring them," she sobbed. "Let's go--to the boat. He must find his own way. Take me." Hurry and fright choked her. "Take me--leave him, if he won't come--I scolded him--then the noises came, and we ran--"

"What boat?" said Rudolph.

Chantel did not look up.

"I have one ready and stocked," he mumbled, tugging with his teeth at the knot in the sarong corners. "You can come. We'll drop down the river, and try it along the coast. Only chance. Come on."

He rose, and started for the door, slinging the bright-colored bundle over his shoulder. "Come on," he snarled. Against the gay pattern, his handsome pirate face shone brown and evil in the lamplight. "Damn you, I've waited long enough for your whims. Stay there and be killed, then."

He ran to the stairs, and down. The woman's arms began to drag loosely, as if she were slipping to the floor; then suddenly, with a cry, she turned and bolted. Run as he might, Rudolph did not overtake her till she had caught Chantel at the gate. All three, silent, sped across fields toward the river, through the startling shadows and dim orange glow from distant flames.

The rough ground sloped, at last, and sent them stumbling down into mud. Behind them the bank ran black and ragged against the glow; before them, still more black, lay the river, placid, mysterious, and safe. Through the mud they labored heavily toward a little, smoky light--a lantern gleaming faintly on a polished gunwale, the shoulders of a man, and the thin, slant line that was his pole.

"Lowdah?" called Chantel; and the shoulders moved, the line shifted, as the boatman answered. Chantel pitched the bundle over the lantern, and leapt on board. Rudolph came slowly, carrying in his arms the woman, who lay quiet and limp, clasping him in a kind of drowsy oblivion. He felt the flutter of her lips, while she whispered in his ear strange, breathless entreaties, a broken murmur of endearments, unheard-of, which tempted him more than the wide, alluring darkness of the river.

He lowered her slowly; and leaning against the gunwale, she still clung to his hands.

"Aboard! Quickly!" snapped their leader, from the dusk behind the lantern.

Obeying by impulse, Rudolph moved nearer the gunwale. The slippery edge, polished by bare feet through many years, seemed the one bit of reality in this dream, except the warmth of her hands.

"To the nunnery?" he asked, trying dully to rouse from a

fascination.

"No, no," she wailed. "Down--away--safe."

"No, back to them," he answered stupidly. "They are all there. Your--he is there. We can't leave--"

"You fool!" Chantel swore in one tongue, and in another cried to the boatman--"Shove off, if they won't come!" He seized the woman roughly and pulled her on board; but she reached out and caught Rudolph's hand again.

"Come, hurry," she whispered, tugging at him. "Come, dear boy. I won't leave you. Quickly. You saw it burning. They're all dead. It's no use. We must live. We must live, darling."

She was right, somehow; there was no power to confute her. He must come with her, or run back, useless, into the ring of swords and flames. She and life were in the boat; ashore, a friend cut off beyond reach, an impossible duty, and death. His eyes, dull and fixed in the smoky lantern-light, rested for an age on the knotted sarong. It meant nothing; then in a flash, as though for him all light of the eyes had concentrated in a single vision, it meant everything. The colored cloth--rudely painted in the hut of some forgotten mountaineer--held all her treasure and her heart, the things of this world. She must go with those. It was fitting. She was beautiful--in all her fear and disorder, still more beautiful. She went with life, departing into a dream. This glossy gunwale, polished by bare feet, was after all the sole reality, a shining line between life and death.

"Then I must die," he groaned, and wrenched his hands away from that perilous boundary.

He vaguely heard her cry out, vaguely saw Chantel rise above the lantern and slash down at him with the lowdah's pole. The bamboo struck him, heavy but glancing, on the head. He staggered, lost his footing, and fell into the mud, where, as though his choice had already overtaken him, he lay without thought or emotion, watching the dim light float off into the darkness.

By and by it was gone. From somewhere in another direction came a sharp, continual, crackling fusillade, like the snapping of dry bamboo-joints in a fire. The unstirring night grew heavier with the smell of burnt gunpowder. But

Rudolph, sitting in the mud, felt only that his eyes were dry and leaden in their sockets, that there was a drumming in his ears, and that if heat and weariness thus made an end of him, he need no longer watch the oppressive multitude of stars, or hear the monotony of flowing water.

Something stirred in the dry grass above him. Without turning, he heard a man scramble down the bank; without looking up, he felt some one pause and stoop close. When at last, in profound apathy, he raised his eyes, he saw against the starlight the hat, head, and shoulders of a coolie.

Quite natural, he thought, that the fellow should be muttering in German. It was only the halting, rusty fashion of the speech that finally fretted him into listening. The words did not concern him.

"Are you dead, then?" grumbled the coolie. "Did she kill you?"

Rudolph dismissed him with a vague but angry motion.

Some time afterward the same voice came louder. The coolie was still there.

"You cannot sit here all night," he said. "By daylight they will catch you. Come. Perhaps I can take you to your friends. Come."

Rudolph felt sharp knuckles working at his lips, and before he could rebel, found his mouth full of sweet fiery liquid. He choked, swallowed, and presently heard the empty bottle splash in the river.

"*Stösst an!*" said the rescuer, and chuckled something in dispraise of women. "Is that not better?"

The rice-brandy was hot and potent; for of a sudden Rudolph found himself afoot and awake. A dizzy warmth cleared his spirit. He understood perfectly. This man, for some strange reason, was Wutzler, a coolie and yet a brother from the fatherland. He and his nauseous alien brandy had restored the future. There was more to do.

"Come on." The forsaken lover was first man up the bank. "See!" he cried, pointing to a new flare in the distance. The whole region was now aglow like a furnace, and filled with smoke, with prolonged yells, and a continuity of explosions that ripped the night air like tearing silk. "Her house is burning now."

"You left in time." Wutzler shuffled before him, with the trot of a lean and exhausted laborer. "I was with the men you fought, when you ran. I followed to the house, and then here, to the river. I was glad you did not jump on board." He glanced back, timidly, for approbation. "I am a great coward, Herr Heywood told me so,--but I also stay and help."

He steered craftily among the longest and blackest shadows, now jogging in a path, now threading the boundary of a rice-field, or waiting behind trees; and all the time, though devious and artful as a deer-stalker, crept toward the centre of the noise and the leaping flames. When the quaking shadows grew thin and spare, and the lighted clearings dangerously wide, he swerved to the right through a rolling bank of smoke. They coughed as they ran.

Once Rudolph paused, with the heat of the fire on his cheeks.

"The nunnery is burning," he said hopelessly.

His guide halted, peered shrewdly, and listened.

"No, they are still shooting," he answered, and limped onward, skirting the uproar.

At last, when by pale stars above the smoke and flame and sparks, Rudolph judged that they were somewhere north of the nunnery, they came stumbling down into a hollow encumbered with round, swollen obstacles. Like a patch of enormous melons, oil-jars lay scattered.

"Hide here, and wait," commanded Wutzler. "I will go see." And he flitted off through the smoke.

Smuggled among the oil-jars, Rudolph lay panting. Shapes of men ran past, another empty jar rolled down beside him, and a stray bullet sang overhead like a vibrating wire. Soon afterward, Wutzler came crawling through the huddled pottery.

"Lie still," he whispered. "Your friends are hemmed in. You cannot get through."

The smell of rancid oil choked them, yet they could breathe without coughing, and could rest their smarting eyes. In the midst of tumult and combustion, the hollow lay dark as a pool. Along its rim bristled a scrubby fringe of weeds, black against a rosy cloud.

After a time, something still blacker parted the weeds. In silhouette, a man's head, his hand grasping a staff or the muzzle of a gun, remained there as still as though, crawling to the verge, he lay petrified in the act of spying.

CHAPTER XVII

LAMP OF HEAVEN

The white men peered from among the oil-jars, like two of the Forty Thieves. They could detect no movement, friendly or hostile: the black head lodged there without stirring. The watcher, whether he had seen them or not, was in no hurry; for with chin propped among the weeds, he held a pose at once alert and peaceful, mischievous and leisurely, as though he were master of that hollow, and might lie all night drowsing or waking, as the humor prompted.

Wutzler pressed his face against the earth, and shivered in the stifling heat. The uncertainty grew, with Rudolph, into an acute distress. His legs ached and twitched, the bones of his neck were stretched as if to break, and a corner of broken clay bored sharply between his ribs. He felt no fear, however: only a great impatience to have the spy begin,-- rise, beckon, call to his fellows, fire his gun, hit or miss.

This longing, or a flash of anger, or the rice-brandy working so nimbly in his wits, gave him both impulse and plan.

"Don't move," he whispered; "wait here." And wriggling backward, inch by inch, feet foremost among the crowded bellies of the jars, he gained the further darkness. So far as sight would carry, the head stirred no more than if it had been a cannon-ball planted there on the verge, against the rosy cloud. From crawling, Rudolph rose to hands and knees, and silently in the dust began to creep on a long circuit. Once, through a rift in smoke, he saw a band of yellow musketeers, who crouched behind some ragged earthwork or broken wall, loading and firing without pause or care, chattering like outraged monkeys, and all too busy to spare a glance behind. Their heads bobbed up and down in queer scarlet turbans or scarfs, like the flannel nightcaps of so many diabolic invalids.

Passing them unseen, he crept back toward his hollow. In spite of smoke, he had gauged and held his circle nicely, for straight ahead lay the man's legs. Taken thus in the rear, he still lay prone, staring down the slope, inactive; yet legs, body, and the bent arm that clutched a musket beside him in the grass, were stiff with some curious excitement. He seemed ready to spring up and fire.

No time to lose, thought Rudolph; and rising, measured his distance with a painful, giddy exactness. He would have counted to himself before leaping, but his throat was too dry. He flinched a little, then shot through the air, and landed heavily, one knee on each side, pinning the fellow down as he grappled underneath for the throat. Almost in the same movement he had bounded on foot again, holding both hands above his head, as high as he could withdraw them. The body among the weeds lay cold, revoltingly indifferent to stratagem or violence, in the same tense attitude, which had nothing to do with life.

Rudolph dropped his hands, and stood confounded by his own brutal discourtesy. Wutzler, crawling out from the jars, scrambled joyfully up the bank.

"You have killed him?" quavered the dry little voice. "You are very brave!"

"No, no," cried Rudolph, earnestly. "He was, already."

By the scarlet headgear, and a white symbol on the back of his jacket, the man at their feet was one of the musketeers. He had left the firing-line, crawled away in the dark, and found a quiet spot to die in.

"So! This is good luck!" Wutzler doffed his coolie hat, slid out of his jacket, tossed both down among the oil-jars, and stooping over the dead man, began to untwist the scarlet turban. In the dim light his lean arms and frail body, coated with black hair, gave him the look of a puny ape robbing a sleeper. He wriggled into the dead man's jacket, wound the blood-red cloth about his own temples, and caught up musket, ramrod, powder-horn, and bag of bullets.--"Now I am all safe," he chuckled. "Now I can go anywhere, to-night."

He shouldered arms and stood grinning as though all their troubles were ended.

"So! I am rebel soldier. We try again; come.--Not too close behind me; and if I speak, run back."

In this order they began once more to scout through the smoke. No one met them, though distant shapes rushed athwart the gloom, yelping to each other, and near by, legs of runners moved under a rolling cloud of smoke as if their bodies were embedded and swept along in the wrack:--all confused, hurried, and meaningless, like the uproar of gongs, horns, conches, whistling bullets, crackers, and squibs that sputtering, string upon string, flower upon rising flower of misty red gold explosion, ripped all other noise to tatters.

Where and how he followed, Rudolph never could have told; but once, as they ran slinking through the heaviest smoke and, as it seemed, the heart of the turmoil, he recognized the yawning rim of a clay-pit, not a stone's throw from his own gate. It was amazing to feel that safety lay so close; still more amazing to catch a glimpse of many coolies digging in the pit by torchlight, peacefully, as though they had heard of no disturbance that evening. Hardly had the picture flashed past, than he wondered whether he had seen or imagined it, whose men they were, and why, even at any time, they should swarm so busy, thick as ants, merely to dig clay.

He had worry enough, however, to keep in view the white cross-barred hieroglyphic on his guide's jacket. Suddenly it vanished, and next instant the muzzle of the gun jolted against his ribs.

"Run, quick," panted Wutzler, pushing him aside. "To the left, into the go-down. Here they are!--To your left!" And with the words, he bounded off to the right, firing his gun to confuse the chase.

Rudolph obeyed, and, running at top speed, dimly understood that he had doubled round a squad of grunting runners, whose bare feet pattered close by him in the smoke. Before him gaped a black square, through which he darted, to pitch head first over some fat, padded bulk. As he rose, the rasping of rough jute against his cheek told him that he had fallen among bales; and a familiar, musty smell, that the bales were his own, in his own go-down, across a narrow lane from the nunnery. With high hopes, he stumbled farther into the darkness. Once, among the bales, he trod on a man's hand, which was silently pulled away.

With no time to think of that, he crawled and climbed over
the disordered heaps, groping toward the other door. He
had nearly reached it, when torchlight flared behind him,
rushing in, and savage cries, both shrill and guttural, rang
through the stuffy warehouse. He had barely time, in the
reeling shadows, to fall on the earthen floor, and crawl
under a thin curtain of reeds to a new refuge.

Into this--a cubby-hole where the compradore kept his tally-
slips, umbrella, odds and ends--the torchlight shone faintly
through the reeds. Lying flat behind a roll of matting,
Rudolph could see, as through the gauze twilight of a stage
scene, the tossing lights and the skipping men who shouted
back and forth, jabbing their spears or pikes down among
the bales, to probe the darkness. Their search was wild but
thorough. Before it, in swift retreat, some one crawled past
the compradore's room, brushing the splint partition like a
snake. This, as Rudolph guessed, might be the man whose
hand he had stepped on.

The stitches in the curtain became beads of light. A
shadowy arm heaved up, fell with a dry, ripping sound and a
vertical flash. A sword had cut the reeds from top to
bottom.

Through the rent a smoking flame plunged after the sword,
and after both, a bony yellow face that gleamed with sweat.
Rudolph, half wrapped in his matting, could see the hard,
glassy eyes shine cruelly in their narrow slits; but before they
lowered to meet his own, a jubilant yell resounded in the go-
down, and with a grunt, the yellow face, the flambeau, and
the sword were snatched away.

He lay safe, but at the price of another man's peril. They had
caught the crawling fugitive, and now came dragging him
back to the lights. Through the tattered curtain Rudolph saw
him flung on the ground like an empty sack, while his
captors crowded about in a broken ring, cackling, and
prodding him with their pikes. Some jeered, some snarled,
others called him by name, with laughing epithets that rang
more friendly, or at least more jocular; but all bent toward
him eagerly, and flung down question after question, like a
little band of kobolds holding an inquisition. At some
sharper cry than the rest, the fellow rose to his knees and
faced them boldly. A haggard Christian, he was being fairly

given his last chance to recant.

"Open your mouth! Open your mouth!" they cried, in rage or entreaty.

The kneeling captive shook his head, and made some reply, very distinct and simple.

"Open your mouth!" They struck at him with the torches. The same sword that had slashed the curtain now pricked his naked chest. Rudolph, clenching his fists in a helpless longing to rush out and scatter all these men-at-arms, had a strange sense of being transported into the past, to watch with ghostly impotence a mediaeval tragedy.

The kneeling man repeated his unknown declaration. His round, honest, oily face was anything but heroic, and wore no legendary, transfiguring light. He seemed rather stupid than calm; yet as he mechanically wound his queue into place once more above the shaven forehead, his fingers moved surely and deftly. Not once did they slip or tremble.

"Open your mouth!" snarled the pikemen and the torch-bearers, with the fierce gestures of men who have wasted time and patience.

"The Lamp of Heaven!" bawled the swordsman, beside himself. "Give him the Lamp of Heaven!"

To the others, this phrase acted as a spark to powder.

"Good! good!" they shrilled, nodding furiously. "The Lamp of Heaven!" And several men began to rummage and overhaul the chaos of the go-down. Rudolph had given orders, that afternoon, to remove all necessary stores to the nunnery. But from somewhere in the darkness, one rioter brought a sack of flour, while another flung down a tin case of petroleum. The sword had no sooner cut the sack across and punctured the tin, than a fat villain in a loin cloth, squatting on the earthen floor, kneaded flour and oil into a grimy batch of dough.

"Will you speak out and live," cried the swordsman, "or will you die?"

For a second the Christian did not stir. Then, as though the option were not in his power,--

"Die," he answered.

The fat baker sprang up, and clapped on the obstinate head a shapeless gray turban of dough. Half a dozen torches jostled for the honor of lighting it. The Christian, crowned with sooty flames, gave a single cry, clear above all the others. He was calling--as even Rudolph knew--on the strange god across the sea, Saviour of the Children of the West, not to forget his nameless and lonely servant.

Rudolph groaned aloud, rose, and had parted the curtain to run out and fall upon them all, when suddenly, close at hand and sharp in the general din, there burst a quick volley of rifleshots. Splinters flew from the attap walls. A torch-bearer and the man with the sword spun half round, collided, and fell, the one across the other, like drunken wrestlers. The survivors flung down their torches and ran, leaping and diving over bales. On the ground, the smouldering Lamp of Heaven showed that its wearer, rescued by a lucky bullet, lay still in a posture of humility. Strange humility, it seemed, for one so suddenly given the complete and profound wisdom that confirms all faith, foreign or domestic, new or old.

With a sense of all this, but no clear sense of action, Rudolph found the side-door, opened it, closed it, and started across the lane. He knew only that he should reach the mafoo's little gate by the pony-shed, and step out of these dark ages into the friendly present; so that when something from the wall blazed point-blank, and he fell flat on the ground, he lay in utter defeat, bitterly surprised and offended. His own friends: they might miss him once, but not twice. Let it come quickly.

Instead, from the darkness above came the most welcome sound he had ever known,--a keen, high voice, scolding.

"What the devil are you firing at?" It was Heywood, somewhere on the roof of the pony-shed. He put the question sharply, yet sounded cool and cheerful. "A shadow? Rot! You waste another cartridge so, and I'll take your gun away. Remember that!"

Nesbit's voice clipped out some pert objection.

"Potted the beggar, any'ow--see for yourself--go-down 's afire."

"Saves us the trouble of burning it." The other voice moved away, with a parting rebuke. "No more of that, sniping and squandering. Wait till they rush you."

Rudolph lifted his head from the dust.

"Maurice!" he called feebly. "Maurice, let me in!"

"Hallo!" answered his captain on the wall, blithely. "Steady on, we'll get you."

Of all hardships, this brief delay was least bearable. Then a bight of rope fell across Rudolph's back. He seized it, hauled taut, and planting his feet against the wall, went up like a fish, to land gasping on a row of sand-bags.

"Ho, you wandering German!" His invisible friend clapped him on the shoulder. "By Jove, I'm glad. No time to burble now, though. Off with you. Compradore has a gun for you, in the court. Collect a drink as you go by. Report to Kneebone at the northeast corner. Danger point there: we need a good man, so hurry. Devilish glad. Cut along."

Rudolph, scrambling down from the pony-shed, ran across the compound with his head in a whirl. Yet through all the scudding darkness and confusion, one fact had pierced as bright as a star. On this night of alarms, he had turned the great corner in his life. Like the pale stranger with his crown of fire, he could finish the course.

He caught his rifle from the compradore's hand, but needed no draught from any earthly cup. Brushing through the orange trees, he made for the northeast angle, free of all longing perplexities, purged of all vile admiration, and fit to join his friends in clean and wholesome danger.

CHAPTER XVIII

SIEGE

He never believed that they could hold the northeast corner for a minute, so loud and unceasing was the uproar. Bullets spattered sharply along the wall and sang overhead, mixed now and then with an indescribable whistling and jingling. The angle was like the prow of a ship cutting forward into a gale. Yet Rudolph climbed, rejoicing, up the short bamboo ladder, to the platform which his coolies had built in such haste, so long ago, that afternoon.

His high spirits went before a fall. As he stood up, in the full glow from the burning go-down, somebody tackled him about the knees and threw him head first on the sand-bags.

"How many times must I give me orders?" barked the little sea-captain. "Under cover, under cover, and stay under cover, or I'll send ye below, ye gallivanting--Oh! it's you, is it? Well, there's your port-hole." A stubby finger pointed in the obscurity. "There! and don't ye fire till I say so!"

Thus made welcome, Rudolph crawled toward a chink among the bags, ran the muzzle of his gun into place, and lay ready for whatever might come out of the quaking lights and darknesses beyond.

Nothing came, however, except a swollen continuity of sound, a rolling cloud of noises, thick and sullen as the smell of burnt gunpowder. It was strange, thought Rudolph, how nothing happened from moment to moment. No yellow bodies came charging out of the hubbub. He himself lay there unhurt; his fellows joked, grumbled, shifted their legs on the platform. At times the heavier, duller sound, which had been the signal for the whole disorder,--one ponderous beat, as on a huge and very slack bass-drum,--told that the Black Dog from Rotterdam was not far off. Yet even then there followed no shock of round-shot battering at masonry, but only an access of the stormy whistling and jingling.

"Copper cash," declared the voice of Heywood, in a lull. By the sound, he was standing on the rungs of the ladder, with his head at the level of the platform; also by the sound, he was enjoying himself inordinately. "What a jolly good piece of luck! Scrap metal and copper cash. Firing money at us-- like you, Captain. Just what we thought, too. Some unruly gang among them wouldn't wait, and forced matters. Tonight was premature. The beggars have plenty of powder, and little else. So far."

Rudolph listened in wonder. Here, in the thick of the fight, was a light-hearted, busy commander, drawing conclusions and extracting news from chaos.

"Look out for arrows," continued the speaker, as he crawled to a loophole between Rudolph's and the captain's. "They're shooting arrows up over. Killed one convert and wounded two, there by the water gate. They can't get the elevation for you chaps here, though." And again he added, cheerfully, "So far, at least."

The little band behind the loopholes lay watching through the smoke, listening through the noise. The Black Dog barked again, and sent a shower of money clinking along the wall.

"How do you like it, Rudie?" chuckled his friend.

"It is terrible," answered Rudolph, honestly.

"Terrible racket, yes. Fireworks, to frighten us. Wait till their ammunition comes; then you'll see fun. Fireworks, all this." Heywood turned to his other companion. "I say, Kneebone, what's your idea? Sniping all night, will it be?--or shall we get a fair chance at 'em?"

The captain, a small, white, recumbent spectre, lifted his head and appeared to sniff the smoke judicially.

"They get a chance at us, more like!" he grumbled. "My opinion, the blighters have shot and burnt themselves into a state o' mind; bloomin' delusion o' grandeur, that's what. Wildest of 'em will rush us to-night, once--maybe twice. We stave 'em off, say: that case, they'll settle down to starve us, right and proper."

"Siege," assented Heywood.

"Siege, like you read about." The captain lay flat again. "Wish a man could smoke up here."

Heywood laughed, and turned his head:--

"How much do you know about sieges, old chap?"

"Nothing," Rudolph confessed.

"Nor I, worse luck. Outside of school--*testudine facia*, that sort of thing. However," he went on cheerfully, "we shall before long"--He broke off with a start. "Rudie! By Jove, I forgot! Did you find them? Where's Bertha Forrester?"

"Gone," said Rudolph, and struggling to explain, found his late adventure shrunk into the compass of a few words, far too small and bare to suggest the magnitude of his decision. "They went," he began, "in a boat--"

He was saved the trouble; for suddenly Captain Kneebone cried in a voice of keen satisfaction, "Here they come! I told ye!"--and fired his rifle.

Through a patch of firelight, down the gentle slope of the field, swept a ragged cohort of men, some bare-headed, some in their scarlet nightcaps, as though they had escaped from bed, and all yelling. One of the foremost, who met the captain's bullet, was carried stumbling his own length before he sank underfoot; as the Mausers flashed from between the sand-bags, another and another man fell to his knees or toppled sidelong, tripping his fellows into a little knot or windrow of kicking arms and legs; but the main wave poured on, all the faster. Among and above them, like wreckage in that surf, tossed the shapes of scaling-ladders and notched bamboos. Two naked men, swinging between them a long cylinder or log, flashed through the bonfire space and on into the dark below the wall.

"Pung-dongs!" bawled the captain. "Look out for the pung-dong!"

His friends were too busy firing into the crowded gloom below. Rudolph, fumbling at side-bolt and pulling trigger, felt the end of a ladder bump his forehead, saw turban and mediaeval halberd heave above him, and without time to think of firing, dashed the muzzle of his gun at the climber's face. The shock was solid, the halberd rang on the platform, but the man vanished like a shade.

"Very neat," growled Heywood, who in the same instant,

with a great shove, managed to fling down the ladder. "Perfectly silly attack. We'll hold 'em."

While he spoke, however, something hurtled over their heads and thumped the platform. The queer log, or cylinder, lay there with a red coal sputtering at one end, a burning fuse. Heywood snatched at it and missed. Some one else caught up the long bulk, and springing to his feet, swung it aloft. Firelight showed the bristling moustache of Kempner, his long, thin arms poising a great bamboo case bound with rings of leather or metal. He threw it out with his utmost force, staggered as though to follow it; then, leaping back, straightened his tall body with a jerk, flung out one arm in a gesture of surprise, no sooner rigid than drooping; and even while he seemed inflated for another of his speeches, turned half-round and dove into the garden and the night. By the ending of it, he had redeemed a somewhat rancid life.

Before, the angle was alive with swarming heads. As he fell, it was empty, and the assault finished; for below, the bamboo tube burst with a sound that shook the wall; liquid flame, the Greek fire of stink-pot chemicals, squirted in jets that revealed a crowd torn asunder, saffron faces contorted in shouting, and men who leapt away with clothes afire and powder-horns bursting at their sides. Dim figures scampered off, up the rising ground.

"That's over," panted Heywood. "Thundering good lesson,-- Here, count noses. Rudie? Right-oh. Sturgeon, Teppich, Padre, Captain? Good! but look sharp, while I go inspect." He whispered to Rudolph. "Come down, won't you, and help me with--you know."

At the foot of the ladder, they met a man in white, with a white face in what might be the dawn, or the pallor of the late-risen moon.

"Is Hackh there?" He hailed them in a dry voice, and cleared his throat, "Where is she? Where's my wife?"

It was here, accordingly, while Heywood stooped over a tumbled object on the ground, that Rudolph told her husband what Bertha Forrester had chosen. The words came harder than before, but at last he got rid of them. His questioner stood very still. It was like telling the news of an absent ghost to another present.

"This town was never a place," said Gilly, with all his former steadiness,--"never a place to bring a woman. And--and of her age."

All three men listened to the conflict of gongs and crackers, and to the shouting, now muffled and distant behind the knoll. All three, as it seemed to Rudolph, had consented to ignore something vile.

"That's all I wanted to know," said the older man, slowly. "I must get back to my post. You didn't say, but--She made no attempt to come here? Well, that's--that's lucky. I'll go back."

For some time again they stood as though listening, till Heywood spoke:--

"Holding your own, are you, by the water gate?"

"Oh, yes," replied Forrester, rousing slightly. "All quiet there. No more arrows. Converts behaving splendidly. Two or three have begged for guns."

"Give 'em this." Heywood skipped up the ladder, to return with a rifle. "And this belt--Kempner's. Poor chap, he'll never ask you to return them.--Anything else?"

"No," answered Gilly, taking the dead man's weapon, and moving off into the darkness. "No, except "--He halted. "Except if we come to a pinch, and need a man for some tight place, then give me first chance. Won't you? I could do better, now, than--than you younger men. Oh, and Hackh; your efforts to-night--Well, few men would have dared, and I feel immensely grateful."

He disappeared among the orange trees, leaving Rudolph to think about such gratitude.

"Now, then," called Heywood, and stooped to the white bundle at their feet. "Don't stand looking. Can't be helped. Trust old Gilly to take it like a man. Come bear a hand."

And between them the two friends carried to the nunnery a tiresome theorist, who had acted once, and now, himself tired and limp, would offend no more by speaking.

When the dawn filled the compound with a deep blue

twilight, and this in turn grew pale, the night-long menace of noise gradually faded also, like an orgy of evil spirits dispersing before cockcrow. To ears long deafened, the wide stillness had the effect of another sound, never heard before. Even when disturbed by the flutter of birds darting from top to dense green top of the orange trees, the air seemed hushed by some unholy constraint. Through the cool morning vapors, hot smoke from smouldering wreckage mounted thin and straight, toward where the pale disk of the moon dissolved in light. The convex field stood bare, except for a few overthrown scarecrows in naked yellow or dusty blue, and for a jagged strip of earthwork torn from the crest, over which the Black Dog thrust his round muzzle. In a truce of empty silence, the defenders slept by turns among the sand-bags.

The day came, and dragged by without incident. The sun blazed in the compound, swinging overhead, and slanting down through the afternoon. At the water gate, Rudolph, Heywood, and the padre, with a few forlorn Christians,-- driven in like sheep, at the last moment,--were building a rough screen against the arrows that had flown in darkness, and that now lay scattered along the path. One of these a workman suddenly caught at, and with a grunt, held up before the padre.

The head was blunt. About the shaft, wound tightly with silk thread, ran a thin roll of Chinese paper.

Dr. Earle nodded, took the arrow, and slitting with a pocket-knife, freed and flattened out a painted scroll of complex characters. His keen old eyes ran down the columns. His face, always cloudy now, grew darker with perplexity.

"A message," he declared slowly. "I think a serious message." He sat down on a pile of sacks, and spread the paper on his knee. "But the characters are so elaborate--I can't make head or tail."

He beckoned Heywood, and together they scowled at the intricate and meaningless symbols.

"All alike," complained the younger man. "Maddening." Then his face lighted. "No, see here--lower left hand."

The last stroke of the brush, down in the corner, formed a loose "O. W."

"From Wutzler. Must mean something."

For all that, the painted lines remained a stubborn puzzle.

"Something, yes. But what?" The padre pulled out a cigar, and smoking at top speed, spaced off each character with his thumb. "They are all alike, and yet"--He clutched his white hair with big knuckles, and tugged; replaced his mushroom helmet; held the paper at a new focus. "Ah!" he said doubtfully; and at last, "Yes." For some time he read to himself, nodding. "A Triad cipher."

"Well?" resumed Heywood, patiently.

The reader pointed with his cigar.

"Take only the left half of that word, and what have you?"

"'Lightning,'" read Heywood.

"The right half?"

"'Boat.'"

"Take," the padre ordered, "this one; left half?"

"'Lightning,'" repeated his pupil. "The right half--might be 'rice-scoop,' But that's nonsense."

"No," said the padre. "You have the secret. It's good Triad writing. Subtract this twisted character 'Lightning' from each, and we've made the crooked straight. The writer was afraid of being caught. Here's the sense of his message, I take it." And he read off, slowly:--

"A Hakka boat on opposite shore; a green flag and a rice-scoop hoisted at her mast; light a fire on the water-gate steps, and she will come quickly, day or night.--O.W."

Heywood took the news coldly. He shook his head, and stood thinking.

"That won't help," he said curtly. "Never in the world."

With the aid of a convert, he unbarred the ponderous gate, and ventured out on the highest slab of the landing-steps. Across the river, to be sure, there lay--between a local junk and a stray *papico* from the north--the high-nosed Hakka boat, her deck roofed with tawny basket-work, and at her masthead a wooden rice-measure dangling below a green rag. Aft, by the great steering-paddle, perched a man, motionless, yet seeming to watch. Heywood turned, however, and pointed downstream to where, at the bend of the river, a little spit of mud ran out from the marsh. On the spit, from among tussocks, a man in a round hat sprang up like a thin black toadstool. He waved an arm, and gave a shrill cry, summoning help from further inland. Other hats presently came bobbing toward him, low down among the marsh. Puffs of white spurted out from the mud. And as Heywood dodged back through the gate, and Nesbit's rifle answered from his little fort on the pony-shed, the distant crack of the muskets joined with a spattering of ooze and a chipping of stone on the river-stairs.

"Covered, you see," said Heywood, replacing the bar. "Last resort, perhaps, that way. Still, we may as well keep a bundle of firewood ready here."

The shots from the marsh, though trivial and scattering, were like a signal; for all about the nunnery, from a ring of hiding-places, the noise of last night broke out afresh. The sun lowered through a brown, burnt haze, the night sped up from the ocean, covering the sky with sudden darkness, in which stars appeared, many and cool, above the torrid earth and the insensate turmoil. So, without change but from pause to outbreak, outbreak to pause, nights and days went by in the siege.

Nothing happened. One morning, indeed, the fragments of another blunt arrow came to light, broken underfoot and trampled into the dust. The paper scroll, in tatters, held only a few marks legible through dirt and heel-prints: "Listen-- work fast--many bags--watch closely." And still nothing happened to explain the warning.

That night Heywood even made a sortie, and stealing from the main gate with four coolies, removed to the river certain relics that lay close under the wall, and would soon become intolerable. He had returned safely, with an ancient musket, a bag of bullets, a petroleum squirt, and a small bundle of pole-axes, and was making his tour of the defenses, when he stumbled over Rudolph, who knelt on the ground under what in old days had been the chapel, and near what now was Kempner's grave.

He was not kneeling in devotion, for he took Heywood by the arm, and made him stoop.

"I was coming," he said, "to find you. The first night, I saw coolies working in the clay-pit. Bend, a moment over. Put now the ear close,"

Heywood laid his cheek in the dust.

"They're keeping such a racket outside," he muttered; and then, half to himself: "It certainly is. Rudie, it's--it's as if poor Kempner were--waking up." He listened again. "You're right. They are digging."

The two friends sat up, and eyed each other in the starlight.

CHAPTER XIX

BROTHER MOLES

This new danger, working below in the solid earth, had thrown Rudolph into a state of sullen resignation. What was the use now, he thought indignantly, of all their watching and fighting? The ground, at any moment, might heave, break, and spring up underfoot. He waited for his friend to speak out, and put the same thought roundly into words. Instead, to his surprise, he heard something quite contrary.

"Now we know!" said Heywood, in lively satisfaction. "Now we know what the beasts have up their sleeve. That's a comfort. Rather!"

He sat thinking, a white figure in the starlight, cross-legged like a Buddha.

"That's why they've all been lying doggo," he continued. "And then their bad marksmanship, with all this sniping-- they don't care, you see, whether they pot us or not. They'd rather make one clean sweep, and 'blow us at the moon.' Eh? Cheer up, Rudie: so long as they're digging, they're not blowing. Are they?"

While he spoke, the din outside the walls wavered and sank, at last giving place to a shrill, tiny interlude of insect voices. In this diluted silence came now and then a tinkle of glass from the dark hospital room where Miss Drake was groping among her vials. Heywood listened.

"If it weren't for that," he said quietly, "I shouldn't much care. Except for the women, this would really be great larks." Then, as a shadow flitted past the orange grove, he roused himself to hail: "Ah Pat! Go catchee four piecee coolie-man!"

"Can do." The shadow passed, and after a time returned with four other shadows. They stood waiting, till Heywood raised his head from the dust.

"Those noises have stopped, down there," he said to Rudolph; and rising, gave his orders briefly. The coolies were to dig, strike into the sappers' tunnel, and report at once: "Chop-chop.--Meantime, Rudie, let's take a holiday. We can smoke in the courtyard."

A solitary candle burned in the far corner of the inclosure, and cast faint streamers of reflection along the wet flags, which, sluiced with water from the well, exhaled a slight but grateful coolness. Heywood stooped above the quivering flame, lighted a cigar, and sinking loosely into a chair, blew the smoke upward in slow content.

"Luxury!" he yawned. "Nothing to do, nothing to fret about, till the compradore reports. Wonderful--too good to be true."

For a long time, lying side by side, they might have been asleep. Through the dim light on the white walls dipped and swerved the drunken shadow of a bat, who now whirled as a flake of blackness across the stars, now swooped and set the humbler flame reeling. The flutter of his leathern wings, and the plash of water in the dark, where a coolie still drenched the flags, marked the sleepy, soothing measures in a nocturne, broken at strangely regular intervals by a shot, and the crack of a bullet somewhere above in the deserted chambers.

"Queer," mused Heywood, drowsily studying his watch. "The beggar puts one shot every five minutes through the same window.--I wonder what he's thinking about? Lying out there, firing at the Red-Bristled Ghosts. Odd! Wonder what they're all"--He put back his cigar, mumbling. "Handful of poor blackguards, all upset in their minds, and sweating round. And all the rest tranquil as ever, eh?--the whole country jogging on the same old way, or asleep and dreaming dreams, perhaps, same kind of dreams they had in Marco Polo's day."

The end of his cigar burned red again; and again, except for that, he might have been asleep. Rudolph made no answer, but lay thinking. This brief moment of rest in the cool, dim courtyard--merely to lie there and wait--seemed precious above all other gain or knowledge. Some quiet influence, a subtle and profound conviction, slowly was at work in him. It was patience, wonder, steady confidence,--all three, and more. He had felt it but this once, obscurely; might die without knowing it in clearer fashion; and yet could never lose it, or forget, or come to any later harm. With it the stars, above the dim vagaries of the bat, were brightly interwoven. For the present he had only to lie ready, and wait, a single comrade in a happy army.

Through a dark little door came Miss Drake, all in white, and moving quietly, like a symbolic figure of evening, or the genius of the place. Her hair shone duskily as she bent beside the candle, and with steady fingers tilted a vial, from which amber drops fell slowly into a glass. With dark eyes watching closely, she had the air of a young, beneficent Medea, intent on some white magic.

"Aren't you coming," called Heywood, "to sit with us awhile?"

"Can't, thanks," she replied, without looking up. "I'm too busy."

"That's no excuse. Rest a little."

She moved away, carrying her medicines, but paused in the door, smiled back at him as from a crypt, and said:--

"Have *you* been hurt?"

"Only my feelings."

"I've no time," she laughed, "for lazy able-bodied persons." And she was gone in the darkness, to sit by her wounded men.

With her went the interval of peace; for past the well-curb came another figure, scuffing slowly toward the light. The compradore, his robes lost in their background, appeared as an oily face and a hand beckoning with downward sweep. The two friends rose, and followed him down the courtyard. In passing out, they discovered the padre's wife lying exhausted in a low chair, of which she filled half the length and all the width. Heywood paused beside her with some friendly question, to which Rudolph caught the answer.

"Oh, quite composed." Her voice sounded fretful, her fan stirred weakly. "Yes, wonderfully composed. I feel quite ready to suffer for the faith."

"Dear Mrs. Earle," said the young man, gently, "there ought to be no need. Nobody shall suffer, if we can prevent. I think we can."

Under the orange trees, he laid an unsteady hand on Rudolph's arm, and halting, shook with quiet merriment.

"Poor dear lady!" he whispered, and went forward chuckling.

Loose earth underfoot warned them not to stumble over the new-raised mound beside the pit, which yawned slightly blacker than the night. Kempner's grave had not been quieter. The compradore stood whispering: they had found the tunnel empty, because, he thought, the sappers were gone out to eat their chow.

"We'll see, anyway," said Heywood, stripping off his coat. He climbed over the mound, grasped the edges, and promptly disappeared. In the long moment which followed, the earth might have closed on him. Once, as Rudolph bent listening over the shaft, there seemed to come a faint momentary gleam; but no sound, and no further sign, until the head and shoulders burrowed up again.

"Big enough hole down there," he reported, swinging clear, and sitting with his feet in the shaft. "Regular cave. Three sacks of powder stowed already, so we're none too soon.-- One sack was leaky. I struck a match, and nearly blew myself to Casabianca." He paused, as if reflecting. "It gives us a plan, though. Rudie: are you game for something rather foolhardy? Be frank, now; for if you wouldn't really enjoy it, I'll give old Gilly Forrester his chance."

"No!" said Rudolph, stung as by some perfidy. "You make me--ashamed! This is all ours, this part, so!"

"Can do," laughed the other. "Get off your jacket. Give me half a moment start, so that you won't jump on my head." And he went wriggling down into the pit.

An unwholesome smell of wet earth, a damp, subterranean coolness, enveloped Rudolph as he slid down a flue of greasy clay, and stooping, crawled into the horizontal bore of the tunnel. Large enough, perhaps, for two or three men to pass on all fours, it ran level, roughly cut, through earth wet with seepage from the river, but packed into a smooth floor by many hands and bare knees. It widened suddenly before him. In the small chamber of the mine, choked with the smell of stale betel, he bumped Heywood's elbow.

"Some Fragrant Ones have been working here, I should say." The speaker patted the ground with quick palms, groping. "Phew! They've worked like steam. This explains old Wutz, and his broken arrow. I say, Rudie, feel about. I saw a coil of fuse lying somewhere.--At least, I thought it was. Ah, never mind: have-got!" He pulled something along the floor. "How's the old forearm I gave you? I forgot that. Equal to hauling a sack out? Good! Catch hold, here."

Sweeping his hand in the darkness, he captured Rudolph's, and guided it to where a powder-bag lay.

"Now, then, carry on," he commanded; and crawling into the tunnel, flung back fragments of explanation as he tugged at his own load. "Carry these out--far as we dare--touch 'em off, you see, and block the passage. Far out as possible, though. We can use this hole afterward, for listening in, if they try--"

He cut the sentence short. Their tunnel had begun to slope gently downward, with niches gouged here and there for the passing of burden-bearers. Rudolph, toiling after, suddenly found his head entangled between his leader's boots.

"Quiet," he heard him whisper. "Somebody coming."

An instant later, the boots withdrew quickly. An odd little squeak of surprise followed, a strange gurgling, and a succession of rapid shocks, as though some one were pummeling the earthen walls.

"Got the beggar," panted Heywood. "Only one of 'em. Roll clear, Rudie, and let us pass. Collar his legs, if you can, and shove."

Squeezing past Rudolph in his niche, there struggled a convulsive bulk, like some monstrous worm, too large for the bore, yet writhing. Bare feet kicked him in violent rebellion, and a muscular knee jarred squarely under his chin. He caught a pair of naked legs, and hugged them dearly.

"Not too hard," called Heywood, with a breathless laugh. "Poor devil--must think he ran foul of a genie."

Indeed, their prisoner had already given up the conflict, and lay under them with limbs dissolved and quaking.

"Pass him along," chuckled his captor. "Make him go ahead of us."

Prodded into action, the man stirred limply, and crawled past them toward the mine, while Heywood, at his heels, growled orders in the vernacular with a voice of dismal ferocity. In this order they gained the shaft, and wriggled up like ferrets into the night air. Rudolph, standing as in a well, heard a volley of questions and a few timid answers, before the returning legs of his comrade warned him to dodge back into the tunnel.

Again the two men crept forward on their expedition; and this time the leader talked without lowering his voice.

"That chap," he declared, "was fairly chattering with fright. Coolie, it seems, who came back to find his betel-box. The rest are all outside eating their rice. We have a clear track."

They stumbled on their powder-sacks, caught hold, and dragged them, at first easily down the incline, then over a short level, then arduously up a rising grade, till the work grew heavy and hot, and breath came hard in the stifled burrow.

"Far enough," said Heywood, puffing. "Pile yours here."

Rudolph, however, was not only drenched with sweat, but fired by a new spirit, a spirit of daring. He would try, down here in the bowels of the earth, to emulate his friend.

"But let us reconnoitre," he objected. "It will bring us to the clay-pit where I saw them digging. Let us go out to the end, and look."

"Well said, old mole!" Heywood snapped his fingers with delight. "I never thought of that." By his tone, he was proud of the amendment. "Come on, by all means. I say, I didn't really--I didn't *want* poor old Gilly down here, you know."

They crawled on, with more speed but no less caution, up the strait little gallery, which now rose between smooth, soft walls of clay. Suddenly, as the incline once more became a level, they saw a glimmering square of dusky red, like the fluttering of a weak flame through scarlet cloth. This, while they shuffled toward it, grew higher and broader, until they lay prone in the very door of the hill,--a large, square-cut portal, deeply overhung by the edge of the clay-pit, and flanked with what seemed a bulkhead of sand-bags piled in orderly tiers. Between shadowy mounds of loose earth flickered the light of a fire, small and distant, round which wavered the inky silhouettes of men, and beyond which dimly shone a yellow face or two, a yellow fist clutched full of boiled rice like a snowball. Beyond these, in turn, gleamed other little fires, where other coolies were squatting at their supper.

"Rudie, look!" Heywood's voice trembled with joyful excitement. "Look, these bags; not sand-bags at all! It's powder, old chap, powder! Their whole supply. Wait a bit-- oh, by Jove, wait a bit!"

He scurried back into the hill like a great rat, returned as quickly and swiftly, and with eager hands began to uncoil something on the clay threshold.

"Do you know enough to time a fuse?" he whispered. "Neither do I. Powder's bad, anyhow. We must guess at it. Here, quick, lend me a knife." He slashed open one of the lower sacks in the bulkhead by the door, stuffed in some kind of twisted cord, and, edging away, sat for an instant with his knife-blade gleaming in the ruddy twilight. "How long, Rudie, how long?" He smothered a groan. "Too long, or too short, spoils everything. Oh, well--here goes."

The blade moved.

"Now lie across," he ordered, "and shield the tandstickor." With a sudden fuff, the match blazed up to show his gray eyes bright and dancing, his face glossy with sweat; below, on the golden clay, the twisted, lumpy tail of the fuse, like the end of a dusty vine. Darkness followed, quick and blinding. A rosy, fitful coal sputtered, darting out short capillary lines and needles of fire.

"Cut sticks--go like the devil! If it blows up, and caves the earth on us--" Heywood ran on hands and knees, as if that were his natural way of going. Rudolph scrambled after, now urged by an ecstasy of apprehension, now clogged as by the weight of all the hill above them. If it should fall now, he thought, or now; and thus measuring as he crawled, found the tunnel endless.

When at last, however, they gained the bottom of the shaft, and were hoisted out among their coolies on the shelving mound, the evening stillness lay above and about them, undisturbed. The fuse could never have lasted all these minutes. Their whole enterprise was but labor lost. They listened, breathing short. No sound came.

"Gone out," said Heywood, gloomily. "Or else they saw it."

He climbed the bamboo scaffold, and stood looking over the wall. Rudolph perched beside him,--by the same anxious, futile instinct of curiosity, for they could see nothing but the night and the burning stars.

"Gone out. Underground again, Rudie, and try our first plan." Heywood turned to leap down. "The Sword-Pen looks to set off his mine to-morrow morning."

He clutched the wall in time to save himself, as the bamboo frame leapt underfoot. Outside, the crest of the slope ran black against a single burst of flame. The detonation came like the blow of a mallet on the ribs.

"Let him look! Let him look!" Heywood jumped to the ground, and in a pelting shower of clods, exulted:--

"He looked again, and saw it was
The middle of next week!

"Come on, brother mole. Spread the news!"

He ran off, laughing, in the wide hush of astonishment.

CHAPTER XX

THE HAKKA BOAT

"Pretty fair," Captain Kneebone said. "But that ain't the end."

This grudging praise--in which, moreover, Heywood tamely acquiesced--was his only comment. On Rudolph it had singular effects: at first filling him with resentment, and almost making him suspect the little captain of jealousy; then amusing him, as chance words of no weight; but in the unreal days that followed, recurring to convince him with all the force of prompt and subtle fore-knowledge. It helped him to learn the cold, salutary lesson, that one exploit does not make a victory.

The springing of their countermine, he found, was no deliverance. It had two plain results, and no more: the crest of the high field, without, had changed its contour next morning as though a monster had bitten it; and when the day had burnt itself out in sullen darkness, there burst on all sides an attack of prolonged and furious exasperation. The fusillade now came not only from the landward sides, but from a long flotilla of boats in the river; and although these vanished at dawn, the fire never slackened, either from above the field, or from a distant wall, newly spotted with loopholes, beyond the ashes of the go-down. On the night following, the boats crept closer, and suddenly both gates resounded with the blows of battering-rams. These and later assaults were beaten off. By daylight, the nunnery walls were pitted as with small-pox; yet the little company remained untouched, except for Teppich, whose shaven head was trimmed still closer and redder by a bullet, and for Gilbert Forrester, who showed--with the grave smile of a man when fates are playful--two shots through his loose jacket.

He was the only man to smile; for the others, parched by days and sweltered by nights of battle, questioned each other with hollow eyes and sleepy voices. One at a time, in patches of hot shade, they lay tumbled for a moment of oblivion, their backs studded thickly with obstinate flies like the driven heads of nails. As thickly, in the dust, empty

Mauser cartridges lay glistening.

"And I bought food," mourned the captain, chafing the untidy stubble on his cheeks, and staring gloomily down at the worthless brass. "I bought chow, when all Saigong was full o' cartridges!"

The sight of the spent ammunition at their feet gave them more trouble than the swarming flies, or the heat, or the noises tearing and splitting the heat. Even Heywood went about with a hang-dog air, speaking few words, and those more and more surly. Once he laughed, when at broad noonday a line of queer heads popped up from the earthwork on the knoll, and stuck there, tilted at odd angles, as though peering quizzically. Both his laugh, however, and his one stare of scrutiny were filled with a savage contempt,--contempt not only for the stratagem, but for himself, the situation, all things.

"Dummies--lay figures, to draw our fire. What a childish trick! Maskee!" he added, wearily "we couldn't waste a shot at 'em now even if they were real."

His grimy hearers nodded mechanically. They knew, without being told, that they should fire no more until at close quarters in some final rush.

"Only a few more rounds apiece," he continued. "Our friends outside must have run nearly as short, according to the coolie we took prisoner in the tunnel. But they'll get more supplies, he says, in a day or two. What's worse, his Generalissimo Fang expects big reinforcement, any day, from up country. He told me that a moment ago."

"Perhaps he's lying," said Captain Kneebone, drowsily.

"Wish he were," snapped Heywood. "No such luck. Too stupid."

"That case," grumbled the captain, "we'd better signal your Hakka boat, and clear out."

Again their hollow eyes questioned each other in discouragement. It was plain that he had spoken their general thought; but they were all too hot and sleepy to debate even a point of safety. Thus, in stupor or doubt, they watched another afternoon burn low by invisible degrees, like a great fire dying. Another breathless evening settled over all--at first with a dusty, copper light, widespread, as though sky and land were seen through smoked glass; another dusk, of deep, sad blue; and when this had given place to night, another mysterious lull.

Midnight drew on, and no further change had come. Prowlers, made bold by the long silence in the nunnery, came and went under the very walls of the compound. In the court, beside a candle, Ah Pat the compradore sat with a bundle of halberds and a whetstone, sharpening edge after edge, placidly, against the time when there should be no more cartridges. Heywood and Rudolph stood near the water gate, and argued with Gilbert Forrester, who would not quit his post for either of them.

"But I'm not sleepy," he repeated, with perverse, irritating serenity. "I'm not, I assure you. And that river full of their boats?--Go away."

While they reasoned and wrangled, something scraped the edge of the wall. They could barely detect a small, stealthy movement above them, as if a man, climbing, had lifted his head over the top. Suddenly, beside it, flared a surprising torch, rags burning greasily at the end of a long bamboo. The smoky, dripping flame showed no man there, but only another long bamboo, impaling what might be another ball of rags. The two poles swayed, inclined toward each other; for one incredible instant the ball, beside its glowing fellow, shone pale and took on human features. Black shadows filled the eye-sockets, and gave to the face an uncertain, cavernous look, as though it saw and pondered.

How long the apparition stayed, the three men could not tell; for even after it vanished, and the torch fell hissing in the river, they stood below the wall, dumb and sick, knowing only that they had seen the head of Wutzler.

Heywood was the first to make a sound--a broken, hypnotic sound, without emphasis or inflection, as though his lips were frozen, or the words torn from him by ventriloquy.

"We must get the women--out of here."

Afterward, when he was no longer with them, his two friends recalled that he never spoke again that night, but came and went in a kind of silent rage, ordering coolies by dumb-show, and carrying armful after armful of supplies to the water gate. He would neither pause nor answer.

The word passed, or a listless, tacit understanding, that every one must hold himself ready to go aboard so soon after daylight as the hostile boats should leave the river. "If," said Gilly to Rudolph, while they stood thinking under the stars, "if his boat is still there, now that he--after what we saw."

At dawn they could see the ragged flotilla of sampans stealing up-river on the early flood; but of the masts that huddled in vapors by the farther bank, they had no certainty until sunrise, when the green rag and the rice-measure appeared still dangling above the Hakka boat.

Even then it was not certain--as Captain Kneebone sourly pointed out--that her sailors would keep their agreement. And when he had piled, on the river-steps, the dry wood for their signal fire, a new difficulty rose. One of the wounded converts was up, and hobbling with a stick; but the other would never be ferried down any stream known to man. He lay dying, and the padre could not leave him.

All the others waited, ready and anxious; but no one grumbled because death, never punctual, now kept them waiting. The flutter of birds, among the orange trees, gradually ceased; the sun came slanting over the eastern wall; the gray floor of the compound turned white and blurred through the dancing heat. A torrid westerly breeze came fitfully, rose, died away, rose again, and made Captain Kneebone curse.

"A fair wind lost," he muttered. "Next we'll lose the ebb, too, be 'anged."

Noon passed, and mid-afternoon, before the padre came out from the courtyard, covering his white head with his ungainly helmet.

"We may go now," he said gravely, "in a few minutes."

No more were needed, for the loose clods in the old shaft of their counter-mine were quickly handled, and the necessary words soon uttered. Captain Kneebone had slipped out through the water gate, beforehand, and lighted the fire on the steps. But not one of the burial party turned his head, to watch the success or failure of their signal, so long as the padre's resonant bass continued.

When it ceased, however, they returned quickly through the little grove. The captain opened the great gate, and looked out eagerly, craning to see through the smoke that poured into his face.

"The wasters!" he cried bitterly. "She's gone."

The Hakka boat had, indeed, vanished from her moorings. On the bronze current, nothing moved but three fishing-boats drifting down, with the smoke, toward the marsh and the bend of the river, and a small junk that toiled up against wind and tide, a cluster of naked sailors tugging and shoving at her heavy sweep, which chafed its rigging of dry rope, and gave out a high, complaining note like the cry of a sea-gull.

"She's gone," repeated Captain Kneebone. "No boat for us."

But the compradore, dragging his bundle of sharp halberds, poked an inquisitive head out past the captain's, and peered on all sides through the smoke, with comical thoroughness. He dodged back, grinning and ducking amiably.

"Moh bettah look-see," he chuckled; "dat coolie come-back, he too muchee waitee, b'long one piecee foolo-man."

He was wrong. Whoever handled the Hakka boat was no fool, but by working upstream on the opposite shore, crossing above, and dropping down with the ebb, had craftily brought her along the shallow, so close beneath the river-wall, that not till now did even the little captain spy her. The high prow, the mast, now bare, and her round midships roof, bright golden-thatched with leaves of the edible bamboo, came moving quiet as some enchanted boat in a calm. The fugitives by the gate still thought themselves abandoned, when her beak, six feet in air, stole past them, and her lean boatmen, prodding the river-bed with their poles, stopped her as easily as a gondola. The yellow steersman grinned, straining at the pivot of his gigantic paddle.

"Good boy, lowdah!" called Kneebone. "Remember *you* in my will, too!" And the grinning lowdah nodded, as though he understood.

They had now only to pitch their supplies through the smoke, down on the loose boards of her deck. Then-- Rudolph and the captain kicking the bonfire off the stairs-- the whole company hurried down and safely over her gunwale: first the two women, then the few huddling converts, the white men next, the compradore still hugging his pole-axes, and last of all, Heywood, still in strange apathy, with haggard face and downcast eyes. He stumbled aboard as though drunk, his rifle askew under one arm, and in the crook of the other, Flounce, the fox-terrier, dangling, nervous and wide awake.

He looked to neither right nor left, met nobody's eye. The rest of the company crowded into the house amidships, and flung themselves down wearily in the grateful dusk, where vivid paintings and mysteries of rude carving writhed on the fir bulkheads. But Heywood, with his dog and the captain and Rudolph, sat in the hot sun, staring down at the ramshackle deck, through the gaps in which rose all the stinks of the sweating hold.

The boatmen climbed the high slant of the bow, planted their stout bamboos against their shoulders, and came slowly down, head first, like straining acrobats. As slowly, the boat began to glide past the stairs.

Thus far, though the fire lay scattered in the mud, the smoke drifted still before them and obscured their silent, headlong transaction. Now, thinning as they dropped below the corner of the wall, it left them naked to their enemies on the knoll. At the same instant, from the marsh ahead, the sentinel in the round hat sprang up again, like an instantaneous mushroom. He shouted, and waved to his fellows inland.

They had no time, however, to leave the high ground; for the whole chance of the adventure took a sudden and amazing turn.

Heywood sprang out of his stupor, and stood pointing.

"Look there!" he snarled. "Those--oh!"

He ended with a groan. The face of his friend, by torchlight above the wall, had struck him dumb. Now that he spoke, his companions saw, exposed in the field to the view of the nunnery, a white body lying on a framework as on a bier. Near the foot stood a rough sort of windlass. Above, on the crest of the field, where a band of men had begun to scramble at the sentinel's halloo, there sat on a white pony the bright-robed figure of the tall fanatic, Fang the Sword-Pen.

HE WENT LEAPING FROM SIGHT OVER THE CREST

"He did it!" Heywood's hands opened and shut rapidly, like things out of control. "Oh, Wutz, how did they--Saint Somebody--the martyrdom--Poussin's picture in the Vatican.--I can't stand this, you chaps!"

He snatched blindly at his gun, caught instead one of the compradore's halberds, and without pause or warning, jumped out into the shallow water. He ran splashing toward the bank, turned, and seemed to waver, staring with wild eyes at the strange Tudor weapon in his hand. Then shaking it savagely,--

"This will do!" he cried. "Good-by, everybody. Good-by!"

He wheeled again, staggered to his feet on dry ground, and ran swiftly along the eastern wall, up the rising field, straight toward his mark.

Of the men on the knoll, a few fired and missed, the others, neutrals to their will, stood fixed in wonder. Four or five, as the runner neared, sprang out to intercept, but flew apart like ninepins. The watchers in the boat saw the halberd flash high in the late afternoon sun, the frightened pony swerve, and his rider go down with the one sweep of that Homeric blow.

The last they saw of Heywood, he went leaping from sight over the crest, that swarmed with figures racing and stumbling after.

The unheeded sentinel in the marsh fled, losing his great hat, as the boat drifted round the point into midstream.

CHAPTER XXI

THE DRAGON'S SHADOW

The lowdah would have set his dirty sails without delay, for the fair wind was already drooping; but at the first motion he found himself deposed, and a usurper in command, at the big steering-paddle. Captain Kneebone, his cheeks white and suddenly old beneath the untidy stubble of his beard, had taken charge. In momentary danger of being cut off downstream, or overtaken from above, he kept the boat waiting along the oozy shore. Puckering his eyes, he watched now the land, and now the river, silent, furtive, and keenly perplexed, his head on a swivel, as though he steered by some nightmare chart, or expected some instant and transforming sight.

Not until the sun touched the western hills, and long shadows from the bank stole out and turned the stream from bright copper to vague iron-gray, did he give over his watch. He left the tiller, with a hopeless fling of the arm.

"Do as ye please," he growled, and cast himself down on deck by the thatched house. "Go on.--I'll never see *him* again.--The heat, and all--By the head, he was--Go on. That's all. Finish."

He sat looking straight before him, with dull eyes that never moved; nor did he stir at the dry rustle and scrape of the matting sail, slowly hoisted above him. The quaggy banks, now darkening, slid more rapidly astern; while the steersman and his mates in the high bow invoked the wind with alternate chant, plaintive, mysterious, and half musical:--

"Ay-ly-chy-ly
Ah-ha-aah!"

To the listeners, huddled in silence, the familiar cry became a long, monotonous accompaniment to sad thoughts. Through the rhythm, presently, broke a sound of small-arms,--a few shots, quick but softened by distance, from far inland. The stillness of evening followed.

The captain stirred, listened, dropped his head, and sat like stone. To Rudolph, near him, the brief disturbance called up another evening--his first on this same river, when from the grassy brink, above, he had first heard of his friend. Now, at the same place, and by the same light, they had heard the last. It was intolerable: he turned his back on the captain. Inside, in the gloom of the painted cabin, the padre's wife began suddenly to cry. After a time, the deep voice of her husband, speaking very low, and to her alone, became dimly audible:--

"'All this is come upon us; yet have we not--Our heart is not turned back, neither have our steps declined--Though thou hast sore broken us in the place of dragons, and covered us with the shadow of death.'"

The little captain groaned, and rolled aside from the doorway.

"All very fine," he muttered, his head wrapped in his arms. "But that's no good to me. I can't stand it."

Whether she heard him, or by chance, Miss Drake came quietly from within, and found a place between him and the gunwale. He did not rouse; she neither glanced nor spoke, but leaned against the ribs of smooth-worn fir, as though calmly waiting.

When at last he looked up, to see her face and posture, he gave an angry start.

"And I thought," he blurted, "be 'anged if sometimes I didn't think you liked him!"

Her dark eyes met the captain's with a great and steadfast clearness.

"No," she whispered; "it was more than that."

The captain sat bolt upright, but no longer in condemnation. For a long time he watched her, marveling; and when finally he spoke, his sharp, domineering voice was lowered, almost gentle.

"Always talked too much," he said. "Don't mind me, my dear. I never meant--Don't ye mind a rough old beggar, that don't know that hasn't one thing more between him and the grave. Not a thing--but money. And that, now--I wish't was at the bottom o' this bloomin' river!"

They said no more, but rested side by side, like old friends joined closer by new grief. Flounce, the terrier, snuffing disconsolately about the deck, and scratching the boards in her zeal to explore the shallow hold, at last grew weary, and came to snuggle down between the two silent companions. Not till then did the girl turn aside her face, as though studying the shore, which now melted in a soft, half-liquid band as black as coal-tar, above the luminous indigo of the river.

Suddenly Rudolph got upon his feet, and craning outboard from gunwale and thatched eaves, looked steadily forward into the dusk. A chatter of angry voices came stealing up, in the pauses of the wind. He watched and listened, then quickly drew in his head.

"Sit quiet," he said. "A boat full of men. I do not like their looks."

Two or three of the voices hailed together, raucously. The steersman, leaning on the loom of his paddle, made neither stir nor answer. They hailed again, this time close aboard, and as it seemed, in rage. Glancing contemptuously to starboard, the lowdah made some negligent reply, about a cargo of human hair. His indifference appeared so real, that for a moment Rudolph suspected him: perhaps he had been bought over, and this meeting arranged. The thought, however, was unjust. The voices began to drop astern, and to come in louder confusion with the breeze.

But at this point Flounce, the terrier, spoiled all by whipping up beside the lowdah, and furiously barking. Hers was no pariah's yelp: she barked with spirit, in the King's English.

For answer, there came a shout, a sharp report, and a bullet that ripped through the matting sail. The steersman ducked, but clung bravely to his paddle. Men tumbled out from the cabin, rifles in hand, to join Rudolph and the captain.

Astern, dangerously near, they saw the hostile craft, small, but listed heavily with crowding ruffians, packed so close that their great wicker hats hung along the gunwale to save room, and shone dim in the obscurity like golden shields of vikings. A squat, burly fellow, shouting, jammed the yulow hard to bring her about.

"Save your fire," called Captain Kneebone. "No shots to waste. Sit tight."

As he spoke, however, an active form bounced up beside the squat man at the sweep,--a plump, muscular little barefoot woman in blue. She tore the fellow's hands away, and took command, keeping the boat's nose pointed up-river, and squalling ferocious orders to all on board.

"The Pretty Lily!" cried Rudolph. This small, nimble, capable creature could be no one but Mrs. Wu, their friend and gossip of that morning, long ago....

The squat man gave an angry shout, and turned on her to wrest away the handle. He failed, at once and for all. With great violence, yet with a neat economy of motion, the Pretty Lily took one hand from her tiller, long enough to topple him overboard with a sounding splash.

Her passengers, at so prompt and visual a joke, burst into shrill, cackling laughter. Yet more shrill, before their mood could alter, the Pretty Lily scourged them with the tongue of a humorous woman. She held her course, moreover; the two boats drifted so quickly apart that when she turned, to fling a comic farewell after the white men, they could no more than descry her face, alert and comely, and the whiteness of her teeth. Her laughing cry still rang, the overthrown leader still floundered in the water, when the picture blurred and vanished. Down the wind came her words, high, voluble, quelling all further mutiny aboard that craft of hers.

"We owe this to you." The tall padre eyed Rudolph with sudden interest, and laid his big hand on the young man's shoulder. "Did you catch what she said? You made a good friend there."

"No," answered Rudolph, and shook his head, sadly. "We owe that to--some one else."

Later, while they drifted down to meet the sea and the night, he told the story, to which all listened with profound attention, wondering at the turns of fortune, and at this last service, rendered by a friend they should see no more.

They murmured awhile, by twos and threes huddled in

corners; then lay silent, exhausted in body and spirit. The river melted with the shore into a common blackness, faintly hovered over by the hot, brown, sullen evening. Unchallenged, the Hakka boat flitted past the lights of a war-junk, so close that the curved lantern-ribs flickered thin and sharp against a smoky gleam, and tawny faces wavered, thick of lip and stolid of eye, round the supper fire. A greasy, bitter smell of cooking floated after. Then no change or break in the darkness, except a dim lantern or two creeping low in a sampan, with a fragment of talk from unseen passers; until, as the stars multiplied overhead, the night of the land rolled heavily astern and away from another, wider night, the stink of the marshes failed, and by a blind sense of greater buoyancy and sea-room, the voyagers knew that they had gained the roadstead. Ahead, far off and lustrous, a new field of stars hung scarce higher than their gunwale, above the rim of the world.

The lowdah showed no light; and presently none was needed, for--as the shallows gave place to deeps--the ocean boiled with the hoary, green-gold magic of phosphorus, that heaved alongside in soft explosions of witch-fire, and sent uncertain smoky tremors playing through the darkness on deck. Rudolph, watching this tropic miracle, could make out the white figure of the captain, asleep near by, under the faint semicircle of the deck-house; and across from him, Miss Drake, still sitting upright, as though waiting, with Flounce at her side. Landward, against the last sage-green vapor of daylight, ran the dim range of the hills, in long undulations broken by sharper crests, like the finny back of leviathan basking.

Over there, thought Rudolph, beyond that black shape as beyond its guarding dragon, lay the whole mysterious and peaceful empire, with uncounted lives going on, ending, beginning, as though he, and his sore loss, and his heart vacant of all but grief, belonged to some unheard-of, alien process, to Nature's most unworthy trifling. This boatload of men and women--so huge a part of his own experience-- was like the tiniest barnacle chafed from the side of that dark, serene monster.

Rudolph stared long at the hills, and as they faded, hung his head. From that dragon he had learned much; yet now all learning was but loss.

Of a sudden the girl spoke, in a clear yet guarded voice, too low to reach the sleepers.

"What are you thinking of?" she said. "Come tell me. It will be good for both of us."

Rudolph crossed silently, and stood leaning on the gunwale beside her.

"I thought only," he answered, "how much the hills looked so--as a dragon."

"How strange." The trembling phosphorus half-revealed her face, pale and still. "I was thinking of that, in a way. It reminded me of what he said, once--when we were walking together."

To their great relief, they found themselves talking of Heywood, sadly, but freely, and as it were in a sudden calm. Their friendship seemed, for the moment, a thing as long established as the dragon hills. Years afterward, Rudolph recalled her words, plainer than the fiery wonder that spread and burst round their little vessel, or the long play of heat-lightning which now, from time to time, wavered instantly along the eastern sea-line.

"You are right," she declared once. "To go on with life, even when we are alone--You will go on, I know. Bravely." And again she said: "Yes, such men as he are--a sort of Happy Warrior." And later, in her slow and level voice: "You learned something, you say. Isn't that--what I call--being invulnerable? When a man's greater than anything that happens to him--"

So they talked, their speech bare and simple, but the pauses and longer silences filled with deep understanding, solemnized by the time and the place, as though their two lonely spirits caught wisdom from the night, scope from the silent ocean, light from the flickering East.

The flashes, meanwhile, came faster and prolonged their glory, running behind a thin, dead screen of scalloped clouds, piercing the tropic sky with summer blue, and ripping out the lost horizon like a long black fibre from pulp. The two friends watched in silence, when Rudolph rose, and moved cautiously aft.

"Good-night," he whispered. "You must sleep now."

That was not, however, the reason. So long as the boiling witch-fire turned their wake to golden vapor, he could not be sure; but whenever the heat-lightning ran, and through the sere, phantasmal sail, the lookout in the bow flashed like a sharp silhouette through wire gauze,--then it seemed to Rudolph that another small black shape leapt out astern, and vanished. He stood by the lowdah, watching anxiously.

Time and again the ocean flickered into view, like the floor of a measureless cavern; and still he could not tell. But at last the lowdah also turned his head, and murmured. Their boat creaked monotonously, drifting to leeward in a riot of golden mist; yet now another creaking disturbed the night, in a different cadence. Another boat followed them, rowing fast and gaining. In a brighter flash, her black sail fluttered, unmistakable.

Rudolph reached for his gun, but waited silently. He would not call out. Some chance fisherman, it might be, or any small craft holding the same course along the coast. Still, he did not like the hurry of the sweeps, which presently groaned louder and threw up nebulous fire. The stranger's bow became an arrowhead of running gold.

And here was Flounce, ready to misbehave once more. Before he could catch her, the small white body of the terrier whipped by him, and past the steersman. This time, however, as though cowed, she began to whimper, and then maintained a long, trembling whine.

Beside Rudolph, the compradore's head bobbed up.

"Allo same she mastah come." And in his native tongue, Ah Pat grumbled something about ghosts.

A harsh voice hailed, from the boat astern; the lowdah answered; and so rapidly slid the deceptive glimmer of her bow, that before Rudolph knew whether to wake his friends, or could recover, next, from the shock and ecstasy of unbelief, a tall white figure jumped or swarmed over the side.

"By Jove, my dream!" sounded the voice of Heywood,

gravely. With fingers that dripped gold, he tried to pat the bounding terrier. She flew up at him, and tumbled back, in the liveliest danger of falling overboard. "Old girl,--my dream!"

The figure rose.

"Hallo, Rudie." In a daze, Rudolph gripped the wet and shining hands, and heard the same quiet voice: "Rest all asleep, I suppose? Don't wake 'em. To-morrow will do.--Have you any money on you? Toss that fisherman--whatever you think I'm worth. He really rowed like steam, you know."

Rudolph flung his purse into the other boat. When he turned, this man restored from the sea had disappeared. But he had only stolen forward, dog in arms, to sit beside Miss Drake. So quietly had all happened, that none of the sleepers, not even the captain, was aware. Rudolph drew near the two murmuring voices.

"--Couldn't help it, honestly," said Heywood. "Can't describe, or explain. Just something--went black inside my head, you know." He paused. "No: don't recall seeing a thing, really, until I pitched away the--what happened to be in my hands. A blank, all that. Losing your head, I suppose they call it. Most extraordinary."

The girl's question recalled him from his puzzle.

"Do? Oh!" He disposed of the subject easily. "I ran, that's all.--Oh, yes, but I ran faster.--Not half so many as you'd suppose. Most of 'em were away, burning your hospital. Saw the smoke, as I ran. All gone but a handful. Hence those stuffed hats, Rudie, in the trench.--Only three of the lot could run. I merely scuttled into the next bamboo, and kept on scuttling. No: they weren't half loaded. Oh, yes, arrow in the shoulder--scratch. Of course, when it came dark, I stopped running, and made for the nearest fisherman. That's all."

"But," protested Rudolph, wondering, "we heard shots."

"Yes, I had my Webley in my belt. Fortunately. I *told* you: three of them could run." The speaker patted the terrier in his lap. "My dream, eh, little dog? You *were* the only one to know."

"No," said the girl: "I knew--all the time, that--"

Whatever she meant, Rudolph could only guess; but it was true, he thought, that she had never once spoken as though the present meeting were not possible, here or somewhere. Recalling this, he suddenly but quietly stepped away aft, to sit beside the steersman, and smile in the darkness.

The two voices flowed on. He did not listen, but watched the phosphorus welling soft and turbulent in the wake, and far off, in glimpses of the tropic light, the great Dragon weltering on the face of the waters. The shape glimmered forth, died away, like a prodigy. How ran the verse?

"Ich lieg' und besitze.
Lass mich schlafen."

"And yet," thought the young man, "I have one pearl from his hoard." That girl was right: like Siegfried tempered in the grisly flood, the raw boy was turning into a man, seasoned and invulnerable.

Heywood was calling to him:--

"You must go Home with us. Do you hear? I've made a wonderful plan--with the captain's fortune! Dear old Kneebone."

A small white heap across the deck began to rise.

"How often," complained a voice blurred with sleep, "how often must I tell ye--wake me, unless the ship--chart's all-- Good God!"

At the captain's cry, those who lay in darkness under the thatched roof began to mutter, to rise, and grope out into the trembling light, with sleepy cries of joy.